Precision Simplified

For 2/1 Game Force Players

By Neil H. Timm

Order this book online at www.trafford.com
or email orders@trafford.com

Most Trafford titles are also available at major online book retailers.

Note for Librarians: A cataloguing record for this book is available from Library
and Archives Canada at www.collectionscanada.ca/amicus/index-e.html

Printed in Victoria, BC, Canada.

ISBN: 978-1-4269-2430-9

*Our mission is to efficiently provide the world's finest, most comprehensive book publishing
service, enabling every author to experience success. To find out how to publish your book, your
way, and have it available worldwide, visit us online at www.trafford.com*

Trafford rev. 2/19/2010

 www.trafford.com

North America & international
toll-free: 1 888 232 4444 (USA & Canada)
phone: 250 383 6864 ♦ fax: 812 355 4082

Table of Contents

Acknowledgements

I WANT TO THANK my bridge partners, Dave Stentz, John Burbank, Erv Mayhew, Eric Errickson, Bill Amason, and Kay Jones, and my friend, Tommy Solberg, who suggested I write this book. Without their encouragement and helpful suggestions and discussions, it would not have been written.

Finally, I must thank my wife, Verena, who supported me as I sat for many hours in front of my computer typing the material for the book and Marielle Marne for proofreading. However, I am responsible for any errors.

The book reflects our approach to playing Precision. I hope the methods presented within help to improve your game if you currently use some form of Precision, or if not, it helps you to convert to Precision if you play, for example, the 2/1 Game Force System.

Sincerely,

Neil H. Timm, Ph.D.

Silver Life Master

timm@pitt.edu (please e-mail comments and corrections)

Web Page: www.pitt.edu/~timm

December 2009

Introduction

THE 2/1 GAME FORCE System is an improvement over the Standard American System that has been played by bridge players for years. The clear advantage of 2/1 is that it allows a partnership to know that game is possible with only a single bid by the responder. However, a significant disadvantage is that the opener mayhave between 12 and 21 high card points (HCP) when opening one of a suit, obviously a very wide range. To remedy this situation, one may employ the strong club system in contract or duplicate bridge known simply as Precision.

While Precision is still played by many players in regional, national, and international events, many club players shy away from the Precision bidding system since they are afraid of the numerous Alpha, Beta, Gamma, and Epsilon asking bids used in many systems, in particular, Italian Precision. There are countless variations of Precision since its introduction into the bridge world by C.C. Wei of Taiwan in the 1960s. Some go by the name Enhanced Precision, Natural Precision, Clarified Precision, Precision Today, Precision Club (Beginner Intermediate Lounge on Bridge Base Online), The Simplified Club, Incision Forcing Club, Match Point Precision, EHAA (Every Hand An Adventure), and many more too numerous to name.

In Precision, the opening suit bids of one diamond, one heart, and one spade are all natural, with the restriction that the hand is now limited to no more than 15 HCP. The forcing opening bid is the bid of one club which is similar to the bid of two clubs in 2/1, Standard American, and other standard two club systems. However, the one club opening in Precision has 16+ HCP. While some Precision Systems employ positive direct suit and notrump responses to the one club opening, many others employ transfer bids to ensure that the strong hand plays the contract in order to right-side the contract. And while many variations of Precision have changed the meaning of the notrump opening, the range employed in Wei's original system of 13-15 HCP is common and will be used in this book. Depending on the structure of Precision you adopt, two-level bids like two clubs, two diamonds, and two notrump usually have special meanings, but again are most often limited to 13-15 HCP (there are of course exceptions, the two diamond bid in some systems). The two-level major suit openings are also unique to the variation of Precision you may adopt. However, many systems define them as weak two bids.

I have tried to eliminate the fear of the memory features used by many variations of Precision by presenting a series of bids geared toward simplicity and allow the reader to integrate the Precision bids into their more familiar natural bidding system using the 2/1 Game Force bidding structure that includes combined Bergen Raises, inverted minor suit raises with crisscross, cuebidding, modified scroll bids, and other familiar conventions.

My goal in writing this book is to provide a careful organization of topics so that one may easily convert from any standard two club opening system and in particular the 2/1 Game Force bids to Precision. In the process, one may keep most of his or her natural bidding sequences and the conventions he currently uses with minor modifications.

Bridge is a complicated game. I hope the approach I have taken is useful in the improvement of your game whether you play Standard American, the 2/1 Game Force System, or some other standard two club bidding system.

Even if you choose not to play Precision, the material reviewed may help players understand the bidding sequences employed by Precision players encountered at club games and tournaments.

Chapter 1♣ – The 1♣* Opening

THE STRONG FORCING OPENING bid in Precision is the 1♣*. Even though the bid only occurs about 10 percent of the time, it is the key bid of the system. The bid is artificial, forcing, and shows a strong hand, at least 16 High Card Points (HCP), or at times, a very good 15. Partner is forced to bid, a pass is never an option. When you fail to open a hand 1♣* and instead open it one of a suit (diamonds, hearts, or spades) you are telling your partner that your hand has only 11-15 HCP. Any response by responder to a one-level suit bid is forcing, unless opener bids one notrump (NT). The advantage of Precision over Standard American and the 2/1 Game Force System is that the bids are more precise; hence, the name. An asterisk (*) indicates that a bid must be alerted.

Hand Evaluation in Precision and One-Level Bids

The standard deck of cards for the game of bridge contains fifty-two cards. The cards are organized into suits - spades (♠), hearts (♥), diamonds (♦), and clubs (♣). The sequence spades, hearts, diamonds, and clubs represent the rank order of the suits within the deck. Thus, spades is higher ranking than hearts; hearts is higher ranking than diamonds, etc. The major suits are spades and hearts and the minor suits are diamonds and clubs.

Each suit contains thirteen cards as follows:

A K Q J 10 9 8 7 6 5 4 3 2

The Ace (A), King (K), Queen (Q), Jack (J), and 10 are called honor cards.

A bridge hand is created by dealing the fifty-two cards, one at a time, to four players so that each player has a total of thirteen cards. Partnerships at the game are the two persons sitting North-South, and those sitting East-West. To evaluate the value of your hand, independent of rank, the standard/traditional method promoted by Charles Goren in the late 1940s is to assign values to the honor cards:

Honor	Value
Ace	4
King	3
Queen	2
Jack	1
Ten	0
	10

The evaluation method is referred to as 4-3-2-1-0 point count system. Using this method, one observes that a bridge deck contains a total of 40 HCP. Hence, an "average" hand consists of only 10 HCP.

Playing any contract bridge system where two clubs shows a strong hand (e.g., 2/1 Game Force or Standard American), hand evaluation is a process that should take into account the shape of the hand (hand patterns), honor card combinations, intermediate cards such as 9s and 10s, suit length, and suit quality. Adjusting the point count system to assess the true value of a bridge hand is complicated. A new point counting system that addresses many of these factors is called the Adjust-3 method, proposed by Mr. Marty Bergen, ten-time national champion. Bergen's (2008) "Slam Bidding Made Easier," Palm Beach Gardens, FL: Bergen Books, devotes the first 100 pages to his method. And I have used his approach in my book Timm (2010) "2/1 Game Force a Modern Approach," Trafford Publishing, Indianapolis, IN. However, in Precision, one does not need a complicated system to evaluate bridge hands.

Hand evaluation in the Precision depends on only three factors: HCP, defensive tricks or quick tricks, and the number of losers in the hand.

Before we go into hand evaluation, a hand with a singleton or a void is by definition unbalanced (35.7%). Patterns that do not contain a singleton or a void are 4-4-3-2, 5-3-3-2, and 4-3-3-3 (47.6%) and are called balanced hands; semi-balanced hands are hands with the following patterns: 5-4-2-2, 6-3-2-2, and 7-2-2-2 (16.7%). A frequency table of hand patterns follows.

Common Hand Patterns Arranged
in Order of Frequency

Pattern	Percentage
4 - 4 - 3 - 2	21.55
5 - 3 - 3 - 2	15.52
5 - 4 - 3 - 1	12.93
5 - 4 - 2 - 2	10.58
4 - 3 - 3 - 3	10.54
6 - 3 - 2 - 2	5.64
6 - 4 - 2 - 1	4.70
6 - 3 - 3 - 1	3.45
5 - 5 - 2 - 1	3.17
4 - 4 - 4 - 1	2.99
7 - 3 - 2 - 1	1.88
6 - 4 - 3 - 0	1.33
5 - 4 - 4 - 0	1.24
5 - 5 - 3 - 0	0.90
6 - 5 - 1 - 1	0.71
6 - 5 - 2 - 0	0.65
7 - 2 - 2 - 2	0.51
7 - 4 - 1 - 1	0.39
7 - 4 - 2 - 0	0.36
7 - 3 - 3 - 0	0.27
All Others	**0.69**

Quick tricks (defensive tricks) are evaluated as follows: AKQ = 3; AK = 2, A = 1, AQ=1½, KQ = 1, and K=½.

When counting losers in a bridge hand, one only considers the first three cards in any suit. If any of the three cards **are not** an A, K, or Q, it is considered a loser. With less than three cards, there are these loser honor exceptions: AQ = ½, Kx= ½, KQ = 1, K = 1, Q=1, Qx=2. This is the Losing Trick Count (LTC) method of counting losers.

With these preliminaries, **any bridge hand with 16 HCP, 3+ quick tricks, and usually with no more than five or six losers is opened by bidding 1♣*.**

What about the other one-level bids in Precision?

1♦*	11-15 HCP usually 2+ diamonds, but sometimes only one (alert and if asked explain that diamonds may be short, one or two)
1♥ or 1♠	11-15 HCP and at least 5-cards in the bid major (even though the bids are limited, do not alert)
1NT#	balanced hand, no 5-card major and 13-15 HCP

The notrump range is announced by partner. The pound sign (#) is used to denote that a bid is announced.

Generally speaking, the most important criterion for hand evaluation in Precision is HCP. Next, one determines the number of quick tricks and LTC losers.

When opening one of a suit, a minimum hand in Precision with only 11 HCP should usually contain at least 2½ quick tricks; if a hand does not meet this minimum, it is generally not be opened. However, with a very good hand with intermediaries, it is sometimes reduced to two quick tricks. No hand with less than two quick tricks and 11 HCP should be opened.

With 12-15 HCP, you should open all hands with two quick tricks. Some may modify the criteria depending upon seat location (the third seat). I believe it is best to use the same criteria in all seats whether one is vulnerable or non-vulnerable.

You are dealt the following hands, using the above criteria, what is your bid?

1) ♠ AQ765 ♥ AQJ ♦ 54 ♣ K73

You have 16 HCP, 3½ quick tricks, and 6 losers. Open the hand 1♣*.

2) ♠ AQ7652 ♥ 7 ♦ 54 ♣ AKJ6

You have 14 HCP, 3½ quick tricks, and 5 losers. Open the hand 1♠, showing 5+ spades.

3) ♠ 7 ♥ 976 ♦ AKJ2 ♣ AKQ75

You have 17 HCP, 5 quick tricks, and 5 losers. Open the hand 1♣*.

4) ♠ AJ7 ♥ AQ6 ♦ 72 ♣ Q10963

You have 13 HCP and an essentially balanced hand. Open the hand 1NT. Replacing the J♠ with, say, the 9, what would you bid? Now, the hand has 12 HCP points; however, adding an extra point for the fifth club, you would still open the hand 1NT. Not counting the fifth club, some may open it 1♦.

5) ♠ J9876 ♥ QJ ♦ K54 ♣ A94

This hand has only 11 HCP; however, it does not contain the minimum required two quick tricks, pass.

6) ♠ KQ76 ♥ AQJ9 ♦ K542 ♣ 7

This hand has 15 HCP, 4 quick tricks, and 5 losers. Open the hand 1♣*.

7) ♠ A543 ♥ A76 ♦ A1098 ♣ A7

This hand has 16 HCP, 4 quick tricks and 7 losers. This hand is too strong to open one diamond, and even with seven losers, one must open the hand 1♣*.

8) ♠ AK765 ♥ A9762 ♦ AK10 ♣ void

This hand has 18 HCP, 5 quick tricks, and 4 losers. Again, one would open the hand 1♣*. Playing the 2/1 Game Force System, some may open the hand 1♠; however, you risk the possibility that partner will pass. Using the rule of 44 discussed in Timm (2010), you would open the hand 2♣, which would be equivalent to the Precision opening.

9) ♠ A7 ♥ AKJ874 ♦ AK ♣ KQ5

This hand has 24 HCP, 6 quick tricks, and 3 losers, open the bidding 1♣*.

10) ♠ 765 ♥ A ♦ A10982 ♣ AQJ7

This hand has 15 HCP, 3½ quick tricks, and 6 losers. This is a great hand; however, it has only 15 HCP and 6 losers. You must open the hand 1♦*.

When opening a hand one club, one of a major, one diamond, or 1NT, you should always consider vulnerability. With distributional hands, if you are vulnerable and the opponents are not, you should not stretch your values to open a hand 1♣*. This may stimulate the opponents to enter the bidding and not allow you to describe your hand. If, however, you are not vulnerable and the opponents are, it is sometimes to your advantage to stretch your 1♣* opening bids since the opponents may not be as anxious to enter the auction.

Summary for opening hands 1♣* in Precision

1. **Most all 17+ HCP hands**
2. **Hands with 16+ HCP and 3+ quick tricks and five/six LTC losers**
3. **Any 15 HCP with 3½ - 4 quick tricks, a good five-card suit, and five or less losers**

The most difficult hands in Precision are 4-4-4-1 hands where the singleton is either a diamond or a major and contain 16+ HCP; the frequently used opening is 1♦* (Chapter 10).

Some Final Remarks: When opening 1♣*, we stated that it requires 16+ HCP and a hand with any distribution. Because a negative response by partner with no interference (next chapter) says that partner has between 0-7 HCP, a modification to the 16+ HCP requirements is suggested by some players. The modification is: if the hand is unbalanced and includes at least one four-card major, one may increase the requirement to 17+ HCP. This is done because partner may have only 8 HCP and responds positively; and since 17 + 8 = 25, game may be possible if a major fit is found. With no four-card major and an unbalanced minor suit hand, the requirement for a one club opening is increased to 18+ HCP. These changes, if used, should be discussed with your partner.

Another option, preferred by some, is to instead devalue a balanced hand and require that with a balanced hand one has 17+ HCP to open 1♣*; the balanced hand is devalued for "flatness." With this change, unbalanced hands are then always opened 1♣* with 16+ HCP. Balanced hands with 13-15 HCP are opened 1NT.

Overview of Two-Level Opening Bids

We have reviewed the standard one-level bids; we next turn to two-level bids. While the one-level bids are more or less standard for most Precision systems, this is not the case for two-level bids. Thus, if you say you play Precision, you should review with your partner the definition of your two-level bids. We will employ the following two-level bids.

2♣*	**11-15 HCP and 6+ clubs (not 5), may have a 4-card major**
2♦*	**11-15 HCP and 4=4-1-4/4=4-0-4 in the majors (Modified Mini-Roman)**
2♥ or 2♠	**5-10 HCP and a 6-card suit (vulnerable 2 of top 3 honors, non-vulnerable at least 1 top honor)**
2NT*	**5-5 in the minors and 4-8 HCP non-vulnerable 8-14 HCP vulnerable**

We consider each of these bids and rebids by the opener in future chapters. All 3X level suit bids show 5-10 HCP and a suit with 2/3 of the top three honors when vulnerable, the bid of 3NT* is Gambling (7+ minor AKQJxxx), and finally 4♣* and 4♦* bids are NAMYATS. More on these bids later.

Overview of Responses to 1♣*

After your partner opens 1♣*, as responder, you may not pass. Partner may have as few as 16 HCP, but he could also have a monster hand, with game values in hand. You are required to respond to the forcing one club bid. A summary of the responses partner may make to the strong and artificial 1♣* opening, assuming no interference by the opponents follows. Each will be covered in more detail in future chapters. In some of the entries we refer to controls; they are defined as follows: A = 2 and K = 1.

(1) Negative: 1♦* with 0-7 HCP

(2) Positive Responses -Transfers to MAJORS and NOTRUMP

1♥#	with 5+spades (8+ HCP) opener bids 1♠ with support
2♦#	with 5+ hearts (8+ HCP) opener bids 2♥ with support
1♠#	balanced hand (8-13 HCP) opener bids 1NT (always)

 # announced as a transfer

(3) 1NT*   **3-13 HCP Two 4-card Majors**

(4) 2♣*   **8+ HCP 6-cards in a Minor with 2 of the top 3 honors (may have 4-card major)**

(5) 2♥/2♠   **4-6 HCP and 6+card suit (weak two bids)**

(6) 2NT*   **14+ HCP, balanced hand no 5-card major (Neither partner can pass short of 4NT)**

(7) 3♣*   **1-4-4-4/4-4-4-1 Black Singleton Lacking 4 controls <12 HCP**

(8) 3♦*   **4-1-4-4/4-4-1-4 Red Singleton Lacking 4 controls <12 HCP**

(9)   **(Submarine Strong Singleton Responses)**

3♥*	specifically 1-4-4-4 with 4+ controls (AK+), usually 12+ HCP
3NT*	specifically 4-4-4-1 with 4+ controls, usually 12+ HCP
4♣*	specifically 4-4-1-4 with 4+ controls, usually 12+ HCP
4♦*	specifically 4-1-4-4 with 4+ controls, usually 12+ HCP

(10)   3♠* a solid 7-8 (AKQJxxx) suit, with 12 + HCP with/without side controls

In the above responses to one club, entry (6) is game forcing and (9) and (10) are invitational to game.

Dummy Points in Precision

When you find a seven- or eight-card fit in a major or a minor in Precision, usually with three-card support or with a doubleton honor (for suits), again hand reevaluation is required. As in standard bidding systems, the process is performed by either the opener or the responder. Short-suit points are not used in notrump contracts.

The short-suit dummy or support points are evaluated as follows.

Doubleton	1 point each, always
Singleton	2 points each, but 3 each with 4+ trump
Void	3 or equal to the number of trumps in hand (4, 5, etc.)

Never use short-suit points as the opener or first level responder.

In addition to short-suit points, with a suit fit players may add one point for each trump after five and one additional point for a four-card or five-card side suit. When in a notrump contract, suit length counts and quality side suits count, one may also add an additional point for a six-card suit, two points for a seven-card suit, etc. and yet another for a good four-card or five-card side suit.

9

Chapter 2-Negative Auctions after 1♣* - 1♦*

W HEN PARTNER OPENS THE bidding one club and responder has a weak hand, 0-7 HCP or sometimes a weak 8, responder bids 1♦*. The bid of 1♦* is forcing, and artificial, and must be alerted (*); opener must bid again. Most frequently, the goal is to terminate the auction in a suit contract or notrump usually short of game, a part score. However, partner may also have a very strong hand with perhaps 26+ points so that game of slam may be possible.

Why 7 or 8 HCP? The reason is simple. If partner has exactly 16 HCP, the sum of 16 + 7/8 = 23/24 HCP, game in a major or notrump is less likely unless partner has 17+ HCP. This observation suggests that with a four-card major, the one club opening should have perhaps 17 HCP not just 16+ as suggested in Chapter 1. Then, even with a one diamond response, game is possible in a major suit fit or perhaps notrump.

Exceptions to responding 1♦*

1. If you have 6+ cards in a major and 4-6 HCP **honor values in the major** (e.g., KJ or AJ, but not just an ace), and no four-card side suit, you should not bid 1♦* but instead make a weak jump shift bid of 2♥ or 2♠ (Chapter 5). Partner may have a minimal hand and pass, bid game in the suit you have bid with a fit (usually three cards) and values in the suit, invite game in the major, or invite game in notrump.

2. If you have an ace and king in a 6+ card suit or an ace and king in separate 5-5 or 5-4 card suits, do not bid 1♦*. You must always make a positive response (Chapter 3). This is because these honor cards, aces and kings, represent three controls (A = 2; K = 1). Cuebids by the responder are used to show first or second round controls later in the auction.

Opener's rebids after 1♦*

When partner responds 1♦*, opener makes either natural bids or relay bids. Sometimes you are able to describe your hand with a single bid, but many times it may take several. The schedule of responses follow and for now assumes no interference by the opponents.

Natural suit rebids (non-forcing)

The natural rebids of 1♠, 2♣, and 2♦ show a five- or six-card suit and an unbalance hand with 16-19 HCP. Excluded from the list is the natural bid of one heart. It is used instead as an artificial relay bid so that the opening bidder may more precisely describe his hand (it closely follows the recommendations made by David Berkowitz and Brent Manley [2002] in their book "Precision Today," Memphis, TN: DBM Publications).

Relay, notrump, and forcing bids

1♥* relay bid, responder should bid 1♠*. Opener's next bids (all are alerted except 4NT):

1NT 20-21	HCP balanced may have a five-card major
2♣	5+ hearts, 4+ clubs, non-forcing
2♦	5+ hearts, 4+ diamonds, non-forcing
2♥	5+ heart suit and no extra values
2♠	5+ hearts, 4+ spades, non-forcing
2NT	24-25 HCP balanced hand
3♣/3♦	Forcing, 5-5 in hearts and the suit bid (clubs/diamonds)
3♥	6+ heart suit, invitational to game over the 1♦ bid
3♠	5+ hearts, 4+ spades with extra values
3NT	to play
4♣	6+ clubs, 5+ diamonds, forcing and less than 22 HCP
4♦	6+ diamonds, 6+ clubs, forcing and less than 22 HCP
4♥	to play
4♠	to play
4NT	Blackwood (Asking only for aces, not RKCB)

Partner should not accept the relay by bidding 1♠, but instead bid as follows when the conditions hold.

1NT	5-5 or better in the majors, weak (0-4 HCP)
2♣/2♦/2♥/2♠	modest 6-card suit, weak
2NT	5-5 or better in the minors, weak (0-4 HCP)
3♣/3♦/3♥/3♠	modest 7-card suit, weak

Except for the heart relay bid, opener bids are as follows after the 1♦* bid by partner.

1NT* (shows 16-19 HCP)

This bid shows a balanced hand with 16-19 HCP. This is essentially equivalent to a strong one notrump opening in any standard system. Whatever conventions you use when responding to your 2/1 Game Force System, you would also use playing Precision. For example, Stayman, Puppet Stayman or Modified Puppet Stayman (also called Muppet Stayman), Smolen, Jacoby Transfer bids, Quest Transfers, etc.

2NT* (balanced hand with 22-23 HCP)

The direct response of 2NT has more HCP than the "standard system" opening bid of 2NT, usually 20-21 HCP. The purpose of the Precision bid is to show shape and values. Responses to the two notrump bid in Precision are the same as those used in your 2/1 System. For example, Stayman, Jacoby, and Texas Transfer bids, etc. However, the HCP requirements are modified.

2♠* (equivalent to a 2♣ opener in 2/1 Game Force 22+ HCP)

The bid of two spades shows 5+ spades and at least 22+ HCP. Reponses after this bid would again follow what you would do playing your 2/1 Game Force System.

How does opener show a strong hand in notrump, hearts, diamonds, and clubs after the bid of 1♦* by partner? This is accomplished by using the two heart relay bid as follows.

2♥* relay bid, responder should bid 2♠*. Opener now bids (all are alerts):

2NT	26-27 HCP balanced hand may have a 4-card major
3♥	5/6+ hearts -- equivalent 2/1 bidders 2♣ 22+ HCP (forcing)
3♣/3♦	unbalanced very strong 7+ minor hands (forcing to game 22+ HCP)
4♣/4♦	6-5 (clubs and diamonds/diamonds and clubs) with 22+ HCP

The two heart relay bid always shows a very strong hand in Precision (22+ HCP).

Partner should not accept the relay by bidding 2♠* but bid as follows with less than 3 HCP:

2NT	5-5 two-suited, extremely weak (0-2 HCP)
3♣/3♦/3♥/3♠	modest 7-card suit, extremely weak

3NT* 28+ HCP balanced may have a 5-card major

This bid does not occur very often; alternatively, it may be used to show a very strong Gambling 3NT "like" bid with a long solid minor invitational to slam in the minor or notrump with outside controls. Over the bid of 3NT, one may also use Jacoby Transfer bids.

Responder's rebid after 1♣* - pass - 1♦*- pass -?

Natural suit rebids (non-forcing)

A minor suit rebid of 2♣ and 2♦ by the opener shows a five- or six-card suit and an unbalanced hand with 16-21 HCP. With 0-4 Dummy Points, pass. Game in a minor is not attractive. However, with 5-7 HCP and a balanced hand, you should encourage notrump by bidding 2NT, invitational to game. Partner will either bid 3NT or rebid his minor. If your hand is extremely distribution, say 8-3-2-0 or 7-3-3-1, even with 0-4 HCP, you should bid your seven/eight card suit.

After the major suit bid of 1♠ and only 0-4 HCP and a balanced hand, pass. However, with a fit (3+ card support) and only four/five Dummy Points, raise the bid to 2♠. With 5-7 Dummy Points and 3/4 card support bid 3♠, the double (jump) raise is used to invite game.

If after partner bids 1♠ and you have less than three-cards support with 5-7 Dummy Points, you may introduce your five-card minor suit or your five-card heart suit; otherwise, pass.

We now consider a few hands.

The bidding has gone 1♣* - 1♦* - (2♣/2♦/1♠) - (?), and as responder with the following hands, what is your rebid?

1) ♠ 7 ♥ Q52 ♦ Q534 ♣ J10987

You have 5 HCP.

If opener bids 1♠, you would pass.

If opener bids 2♣, you have 7 Dummy Points (4 HCP and 3 for the singleton spade with 4+ clubs), raise 2 clubs to 3.

If opener bids 2♦, you again have 7 Dummy Points, raise 2 diamonds to 3.

2) ♠ 10987 ♥ QJ6 ♦ J54 ♣ 765

You have 4 HCP.

If opener bids 1♠, you would pass. If, however, the opponents enter the auction, you can show your support later making a competitive bid at the two/three-level, depending on vulnerability.

If opener bids 2♣/2♦, you must pass.

3) ♠ 7 ♥ Q52 ♦ QJ10 987 ♣ Q75

You have 7 HCP.

If opener bids 1♠, without spade support, bid your long suit, 2♦.

If opener bids 2♣, pass.

If opener bids 2♦, you have 7 + 3 = 10 Dummy Points; jump to 4♦.

4) ♠ 7 ♥ K109865432 ♦ 10 ♣ 1096

You have 3 HCP.

If opener bids 1♠/2♣/2♦, you must bid 2♥. With 4-6 HCP, you would not have responded 1♦, bid 2♥ (a weak 2 bid).

5) ♠ QJ ♥ J9876 ♦ K54 ♣ 1094

You have 7 HCP.

If opener bids 1♠, you will invite with a doubleton honor in spades.

If opener bids 2♣/2♦, you might consider bidding 2NT or perhaps 2♥. If partner is balanced he may bid game in notrump (after 2NT) or invite game (after 2♥) by bidding 2NT. With a distributional hand, he would sign off in the minor.

Relay, notrump, and forcing bids

At this point, you may be asking yourself what if openers rebid with five hearts, or if 4-4 in the majors. How does one find a major suit heart fit? For this situation, one either uses the 1♥* relay or 1NT bids. We consider both next; first, the 1NT response by opener.

1NT* (shows 16-19 HCP)

The bid of 1NT* after the bid of 1♦* shows a balanced hand with a hand pattern: 4-4-3-2, 5-3-3-2, or 4-3-3-3 and 16-19 HCP. After the bid of 1NT*, responder becomes the captain of the auction. Because partner may have only 16 HCP, you should not make any invitational bids unless you hold at least 7 HCP since 16 + 7 = 23 and 19 + 7 = 26 (observe that this is equivalent to the requirement that you have between 8 and 9 HCP when playing a standard system and a strong 15-17 notrump since 15 + 8 = 23 and 17 + 9 = 26). For game in notrump, one should have at least 24 HCP and a long suit (5+cards).

When responding to opener's 1NT* rebid in Precision, the methods you employed when playing your 2/1 Game Force are in effect, with minor modifications.

1. With only 0-4 HCP, one would use Garbage Stayman sometimes called Crawling or Creeping Stayman.

2. Use Jacoby four-way Transfers with 0-7 HCP promising at least 5+ cards in the transfer suit.

2♦#	transfer to hearts (♥)
2♥#	transfer to spades (♠)
2♠#	transfer to clubs (♣)
2NT#	transfer to diamonds (♦)

The bids are announced as a transfer. After making the transfer and holding 6-7 HCP, one may invite game in a suit or NT. While some may prefer to use the bid 2♠ as minor suit Stayman and 2NT as an ambiguous transfer to a minor, we discuss instead **Shape Asking Relays after Stayman (SARS)** in Timm (2010), "2/1 Game Force a Modern Approach," Trafford Publishing.

3. With 6-7 HCP, one may use Stayman when 4-4 in the majors or Smolen if 5-4 in the majors (or Quest Transfers). After Stayman, one may also use super-accepts; now, however, the response of 3♦ after 2♣ Stayman shows 19 HCP in Precision.

4. One may modify the Mini-Maxi Convention when playing Precision. The bids are:

3♣*	5-5 in the minors and less than 6 HCP
3♦*	5-5 in the minors and 6 - 7 HCP
3♥*	5-5 in the majors and less than 6 HCP
3♠*	5-5 in the majors and 6 - 7 HCP

I will try not to extend the list to all the possible conventions one may use after the bid of 1NT* by the opener, instead, I hope you can see that the conventions you may use playing 2/1 Game Force or some other standard system, are easily modified to fit into the Precision bidding structure.

We now consider a few more hands. The bidding has gone 1♣* - 1♦* - 1NT* - ? , so what do you bid holding the following hands?

1) ♠ 7 ♥ Q52 ♦ Q534 ♣ J10987

You have only 5 HCP, pass.

2) ♠ 10987 ♥ QJ6 ♦ J54 ♣ 765

You have 4 HCP, playing Garbage Stayman, bid 2♣. If opener bids 2♠, pass. After the bid of 2♦, bid 2♥ which asks opener to pick his best three-cards major. Yes, even hearts.

3) ♠ 7 ♥ Q52 ♦ QJ10 987 ♣ Q75

You have 7 HCP, bid 2NT as a transfer to diamonds. After opener's bid of 3♦, you must bid 3NT with 7 HCP. Do not pass.

If you play four-way transfers with super accepts, you may bid 3♣ showing Kxx or Axx in diamonds, rebid your diamonds to show you have six. Partner now is captain and must decide whether to bid 3NT or game in diamonds. Slam is less likely even having a maximum since 19 + 7 = 26 HCP.

4) ♠ 7 ♥ K10986543 ♦ 10 ♣ 1096

You have 3 HCP, bid 2♦ as the Jacoby Transfer to hearts. After partner bids 2♥, pass.

5) ♠ QJ ♥ J9876 ♦ K54 ♣ 1094

You have 7 HCP and a very nice hand. Again, bid 2♦ as a transfer to hearts. However, after the accepted bid of 2♥, bid 2NT. Partner will bid game in hearts or notrump.

1♥* relay bid, responder (partner) usually bids 1♠*

Playing heart transfers, partner must, with few exceptions, bid 1♠* (alert); the responses by the opening 1♣* bidder are natural, showing 5+ hearts, a two-suited hand or a balanced hand. Opener may have a minimum hand (16-19 HCP) or a strong balanced/unbalanced hand (20-21 HCP).

Partner may refuse a transfer using the following bids:

1NT	5-5 or better in the majors, very weak (0-4 HCP)
2♣/2♦/2♥/2♠	modest 6+card suit, very weak
2NT	5-5 or better in the minors, extremely weak (0-4 HCP)
3♣/3♦/3♥/3♠	modest 7-card suit, extremely weak

Note that if the transfer bid is not accepted, opener is unable to bid 1NT showing a balanced hand with 20-21 HCP and must pass.

With the following hand: ♠ KJ ♥ AK1098 ♦ K109 ♣ Q109, opener has 16 HCP, and using the heart relay procedure, the bidding would go:

Opener	Responder
1♣*	1♦*
1♥*	1♠*
2♥	

The bid shows five hearts and no extra values.

Partner would invite with three hearts or two hearts to an honor with 5-7 HCP. Without heart support and a balanced hand, he would bid 2NT. With a minimal hand, 0-4 HCP, he would pass. Why this complicated structure?

It is a convenient method to show two-suited minimal hands at the two-level. Let's look at another example. Suppose opener and responder have the following hands.

Opener:	♠ Q10 ♥ AKJ109 ♦ AK ♣ J1092
Responder:	♠ K53 ♥ Q78 ♦ Q10987 ♣ 73

Now the bidding would go:

Opener	Responder
1♣*	1♦*
1♥*	1♠*
2♣*	3♦
3NT	

In this bidding sequence, all bids are alerted; even the final bid of two clubs. If asked about the two club bid, explain it as 5-4 in hearts and clubs. After the bid of 2♣*, partner would bid 3♥ and opener would bid 4♥.

If the responder did not have a heart fit but a club fit, then a contract in notrump may be possible. For example, suppose in the preceding example responder's hand was:

Responder: ♠ K53 ♥ 7♦ Q10987 ♣ Q873

Now, with four clubs, the bid by responder may be 3♣ and the opener would be 3NT.

2♥* relay bid, responder usually rebids 2♠*

Playing heart transfers, partner must, with few exceptions, bid 2♠* (alert); the responses by the opening 1♣* bidder are natural. Opener has a hand equivalent to the standard 2♣ opener with 22+ HCP. Partner may refuse a transfer using the following bids:

2NT	5-5 or better in the minors, extremely weak (0-2 HCP)
3♣/3♦/3♥/3♠	modest 7+card suit, extremely weak

Notice that if the transfer bid is not accepted, opener is unable to bid 2NT showing a balanced hand with 26-27 HCP but is forced to bid 3NT. With a distributional hand and 22+ HCP, opener would either, pass, or invite game by bidding 3♥.

The corresponding rebids by the opener (after 2♠*) and partner is as follows (all bids are alerted):

2NT 26-27 HCP balanced hand may have a four-card major

Rebids by partner (responder) are:	
New Suit	shows a king
3NT	0-4 HCP, denies a king
4NT	5-7 HCP, invite slam

3♥ - 5/6+hearts -- equivalent of Standard bidders 2♣ 22+ HCP (forcing)

Rebids by partner (responder) are:	
3NT	0-4 HCP, minimum and no support
4♥	0-4 HCP, minimum and 2-card support

3♣/3♦ - unbalanced very strong 7+ minor hand (forcing to game with 22+ HCP)

Rebids by partner (responder) are:	
New suit	shows king or void
3NT	no king or void
Raise to game	denies king, singleton, or void

4♣/4♦ - 6-5 clubs-diamonds/6-5 diamonds-clubs 22+ HCP

Rebids by partner (responder) are:	
New suit	shows king or void
4NT	no king or void
Raise to game	denies king, singleton, or void

After the sequence 1♣* - 1♦*, and not using the relays, one bids:

2♠* (equivalent to a 2♣ opener in 2/1 Game Force 22+ HCP)

The bid of two spades shows 5+ spades and at least 22+ HCP. Reponses after this bid would follow what you would do playing your 2/1 Game Force System.

2NT* (balanced hand with 22-23 HCP)

> **Rebids by partner (responder) are:**
> With 0-2 HCP   Pass
> With 3-7 HCP   Use your 2/1 bidding structure

Recall that to reach game in either notrump or a suit usually requires between 24-26 HCP. With a long suit, it is possible to bid game with perhaps 24 HCP. Depending on the structure of your hand, you should be able to determine whether to play in a suit or notrump. Slam is again very unlikely.

3NT* 28+ HCP balanced may have a five-card major

> **Rebids by partner (responder) are:**
> 0-3 HCP   pass or 4-level bids are transfers
> 4-7 HCP and balanced   bid 5NT invite slam

ADDITIONAL BIDDING EXAMPLES

We now consider some example hands. The bidding goes: 1♣* - 1♦* - (?), so what are your rebids with each of the following hands?

1) ♠ AQ765 ♥ AQJ ♦ 54 ♣ K73

You have 16 HCP and a minimal hand, bid 1♠ showing your five-card spade suit.

2) ♠A ♥AKQ7652 ♦ AK ♣ AQJ

You have 27 HCP, you would next bid 2♥*, forcing partner to bid 2♠*; next bid 3♥ to show your strong hand and a very good suit. If partner next cuebids 4♣ to show second round control in clubs, a slam or grand slam is possible.

3) ♠ 7 ♥ 976 ♦ AKJ2 ♣ AKQ75

You have 17 HCP, next show your 5-card club suit, bid 2♣. The bid of 4♣ would show 6 clubs and 5 diamonds.

4) ♠ AK7 ♥ AQ6 ♦ A72 ♣ KQ109

You have 22 HCP, bid 2NT.

5) ♠ QJ8 ♥ A9876 ♦ KQ54 ♣ A

You have 18 HCP, after the bid of 1♦*, bid 1♥ and then bid 2♦ to show your shape; 5 hearts and 4 diamonds. You cannot bid 1NT with the unbalanced hand.

6) ♠ AKQ1076 ♥ A ♦ KQ ♣ KQ76

You have 24 HCP, bid 2♠* to show 22 + HCP. Do not jump to 4 spades, partner may have a bust hand.

7) ♠ A ♥ AKQ1076 ♦ KQ6 ♣ AKJ

This hand has 26 HCP, bid 2♥*, forcing partner to bid 2♠*, and then bid 3♥ to show 22+ HCP and your heart suit. If partner cuebids 4♦, slam is possible.

8) ♠ AK765 ♥ A976 ♦ AK10 ♣ 2

This hand has 17 HCP, bid 2♠* to show that you have 4 spades and 5 hearts with a minimal hand.

9) ♠ A7 ♥ AKQ874 ♦ AK ♣ KQ5

This hand has 25 HCP and only 6 hearts, bid 2♥*, forcing partner to bid 2♠* and next bid 3♥. If partner bids 4♣ or cuebids 3♠ to show either the A♣ or the K♠, you would bid 6♥. Or, he may bid 4♥ with no interest in slam.

10) ♠ 765 ♥ A ♦ A10982 ♣ AQJ7

This hand has only 15 HCP, even so, open it 1♣*. Then your rebid is 2♦. You cannot open the hand 1NT. Given the unbalanced nature of the hand, you have to play it in a minor, short of game.

11) ♠ AKJ74 ♥ AKQ ♦ AK ♣ KQ5

You have a balanced 26 HCP; after the bid of 1♦*, bid 2♥* and after the relay bid of 2♠*, bid 2NT.

12) ♠ A ♥ AK ♦ AKQJ1098 ♣ AQ5

You have 27 HCP and long diamonds; after the bid of 1♦*, bid 2♥*, and after the bid of 2♠*, bid 3♦ showing a very unbalanced hand with 22+ HCP and diamonds. If partner raises diamonds, he is denying a king, singleton, or void. However, a new suit would show a king or void. After the bid of 3 diamonds, bid 3NT. After a bid at the 4-level, bid 5NT invitational to 6 NT.

13) ♠ A7 ♥ A ♦ A10982 ♣ AKQJ7

You have 22 HCP and are 6-5 in the minors. Again, use the 2♥* relay bid, but after the bid of 2♠*, you must bid 4♦ to show your 6-5 distribution. A bid of 4NT by partner would deny a king or void and a raise to game in diamonds would deny a king, singleton, or void. Since your diamond suit is weak, you will be satisfied with a game in diamonds.

Similarly, opener bids 1♣* and PARTNER responds 1♦* (0-7 HCP). After opener's rebids of either 1♥*/2♥*, what is your rebid?

1) ♠ 7 ♥ Q5 ♦ Q5342 ♣ J10987

You have 5 HCP and are 5-5 in the minors, bid 1♠*. After the 2-level heart bid, you would bid 3♦. If instead, suppose you were 5-5 in the majors, you would bid 1NT after the heart relay and refuse the transfer. However, after the bid of 2♥*, you would have again bid 3♦.

2) ♠ 10987 ♥ QJ6 ♦ J54 ♣ 765

You have 4 HCP, bid 1♠* after 1♥*; if partner bids 1NT, bid 2♣ (Stayman).

After the bid of 2♥*, bid 2♠* and wait for partner's response.

3) ♠ 7 ♥ J52 ♦ QJ10 987 ♣ J75

You have only 4 HCP; after the bid of 1♥*, bid 2♦ to show your good 6-card suit.

After the bid of 2♥*, accept the transfer by bidding 2♠*. If partner bids 2NT, then bid 3NT. If partner instead bids 3♥, then bid 4♥.

4) ♠ 7 ♥ K1098654 ♦ 1098 ♣ 109

You have 3 HCP, after the bid of 1♥*, bid 2♥; after the bid of 2♥*, bid 3♥. In neither case should you accept the transfer.

5) ♠ 75432 ♥ K10986 ♦ 10 ♣ 109

You have only 3 HCP and 5-5 in the majors; after the bid of 1♥*, bid 1NT, and after the bid of 2♥*, bid 2NT. These bids are used to show the majors.

Responder's rebids after 1♣* - pass - 1♦*- pass - 2♣*

After a negative response to the opening bid of one club, we recommended that one employ the transfer bids of 1♥ or 2♥ as suggested in "Precision Today" to right side the contract. Is there another option? Yes! Instead of the opening one club, bidder showing shape by using the 2♥ heart relay bid with 22+ HCP, Bill Amason recommends that one use the bid of 2♣* as an asking bid. The bid is used to obtain information about partner's high card points or honors. The responses to opener are asking club is as follows:

2♦	0-4 HCP
2♥	no 5-card suit and 5-7 HCP
2♠	yes a 5-card suit and 5-7 HCP
2NT	shows controls: AK, AQ, or KK.

Chapter 3– Positive Auctions after 1♣*

In Chapter 2, we reviewed the one diamond negative response to the strong club opening bid. Positive responses to the 1♣* openings show one of six types of hands: (1) balanced notrump hands, (2) hands with 5+ cards in a major, (3) two-suited hands that are 4-4 in the majors, (4) unusual 4-4-4-1 hands, (5) hands with a 6+ minor, and (6) solid suit hands (AKQ) and at least seven cards; an overview of the positive bids follows.

Positive Responses (notrump and majors)

	1♥#	with 5+ spades (8+ HCP) and support
	2♦#	with 5+ hearts (8+ HCP) and support
	1♠#	balanced hand (8-13 HCP), always
1NT*	4-4 in the majors (8-13 HCP)	
2♣*	6-cards in a Minor with at least 2 of top 3 honors (8+HCP)	
2NT*	Balanced hand with (14+ HCP) and no 5-card Major	

Unusual Positive Responses (these follow "Precision Today" bids)

3♣*	1-4-4-4/4-4-4-1 Black Singleton Lacking 4 controls (8-13 HCP)	
3♦*	4-1-4-4/4-4-1-4 Red Singleton Lacking 4 controls (8-13 HCP)	
3♠*	a solid 7-8 card suit (AKQJxxx), 14+ HCP with or without side controls	

Submarine Strong Singleton Responses (these follow "Precision Today" bids)

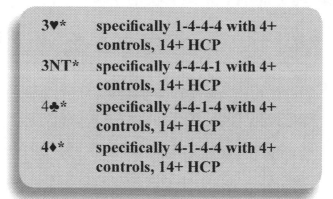

3♥*	**specifically 1-4-4-4 with 4+ controls, 14+ HCP**
3NT*	**specifically 4-4-4-1 with 4+ controls, 14+ HCP**
4♣*	**specifically 4-4-1-4 with 4+ controls, 14+ HCP**
4♦*	**specifically 4-1-4-4 with 4+ controls, 14+ HCP**

3♠* a solid 7+ card suit (AKQJxxx), 14 + HCP with or without side controls

Observe that all positive suit bids involve transfers and excluded from the list are transfers to the minor suits clubs and diamonds. If one has a five-card minor and at least 8+ HCP, we recommend you bid 1♠*, which requires the opener to bid 1NT. Your distribution will be discovered with subsequent bids (details later).

Positive Responses (Notrump and Majors)

Accepting the 1♠ Transfer to Notrump

When partner bids one spade, he has 8-13 HCP and a balanced hand. Opener's responses follow the above structure with balanced hands and no major suit fit.

With a minimal hand, exactly 16-19 HCP, opener bids 1NT* and accepts the transfer. Partner with a four-card major may bid Stayman or pass with a minimal hand. With 9 HCP and no four-card major, bid 2NT.

With 20-21 HCP, opener bids 2NT*. Partner may again bid Stayman or bid 3NT with no four-card major. If partner has 13 HCP, 13+21 = 34 so slam is possible. To invite slam, responder bids 4NT.

With 22-23 HCP*, opener bids 3NT*. Now with a maximum, 13 + 23 = 36, responder bids 5NT as a Grand Slam force.

Accepting the Major Suit Transfer

To accept a major suit transfer, the opening one club bidder must have three-card support or two-card support with an honor.

If opener has a **minimum (16-18 HCP),** the transfer is accepted by bidding:

3♥/3♠ balanced minimum (16-17 HCP), invite game.

With support for the major and 18 HCP, bid game in the major:

4♥/4♠ to play.

If the transfer bid is accepted (opener has 19+ HCP), opener bids 1♠ over 1♥*, and over the 2♦* transfer, bids 2♥. These bids assume no interference by the opponents and are slam tries. Responder next uses (Gamma) control bids to show length when opener accepts the transfer.

The Gamma control bids (GCB) are:

2/3♣*	by responder says I have 5(&)
2/3♦*	by responder says I have 6
2/3♥*	by responder says I have 7

(*) All bids must be alerted

(&) when responder bids two clubs showing only five-cards in the accepted major, opener may bid two diamonds (the next step) to ask about notrump. Responder will bid a suit when at the two-level to show a stopper. 2NT shows stoppers in both minors. A rebid of the five-card major at the two-level shows no stoppers.

Next level bid of the MAJOR at the 2/3 level after Gamma bids are Trump Asking Bids (TAB) used to investigate *trump suit quality*, not controls.

Responses to TAB follow (NT is not used as a step):

Step 1	3/4♣*	no Honors in agreed major
Step 2	3/4♦*	1 top Honor
Step 3	3/4♥*	2 top Honors
Step 4	3/4♠*	3 top Honors

While many books on Precision combine the GAB and the TAB into one series of bids that includes notrump, a series of six responses, we have found them to be too confusing and do not recommend the practice (they are often called TAB or Gamma asking bids).

An important adjunct to Gamma bids (when having 6/7 trump) or the TAB is a new suit (Epsilon) Shortness Asking Bids (SAB) that is initiated by bidding the SUIT. This bid is unique to "Precision Simplified" and will not be found in other versions of Precision. This approach was suggested by Bill Amason and John Burbank.

The SAB is only used to investigate SLAM in a suit and NEVER Notrump.

Responses to Epsilon SAB are (all bids are alerted):

Step 1	no shortness (2+ cards)
Step 2	singleton
Step 3	void

NT is not used as a step "reserved for RKCB"

In many Precision Systems, one uses Control Asking Bids (CAB), also called Beta asking bids. While we will use them on occasion, we do not use them when a fit is established in a major (more on CAB later).

Rejecting the Major Suit Transfer

You cannot accept a major suit transfer if you do not have three-card support or two cards to an honor (A, K, or Q) and an unbalanced or semi-balanced hand. Instead, you must bid your own 5+ card suit (the other major or a minor).

With a balanced hand and no five-card suit, opener bids 1NT* to show 16-19 HCP. Because you may not use the heart relay bids to show 20-21 HCP, the bid of 2NT* is used instead. **Thus, after a positive response it is no longer 22-23 HCP.** If opener has a balanced hand with 22-23 HCP, the bid is now 3NT*.

Responding with Balanced Hands and no major suit fit (all are alerted except 4NT)

1/2NT*	16-19 HCP
2/3NT*	20-21 HCP
3/4NT*	22-23 HCP
4/5NT	24+ HCP

BIDDING EXAMPLES

Your partner opens 1♣*, how do you respond?

(1) ♠ A5 ♥ 109876 ♦ AJ7 ♣ 108

You have 9 HCP and two aces. Bid 2♦# as a transfer to hearts (partner must announce the bid as a transfer; the symbol # is used in the examples as requiring an announcement).

If partner accepts the transfer by bidding 2♥, what is your rebid?

You have only five hearts, bid 3♣*, the GCB (alert and if asked, describe the bid as partner has five hearts).

(2) ♠ A52 ♥ 1098 ♦ AJ7 ♣ 10865

You again have, 9 HCP, but this hand is balanced, bid 1♠# as a transfer to notrump; after partner accepts, bid 2NT.

(3) ♠ AQ76 ♥ AQJ10 ♦ 54 ♣ K7

You are 4-4 in the majors with 16 HCP, bid 2NT*. In general, showing 14+ HCP, the auction cannot stop short of 4NT (more on this shortly).

(4) ♠ KQ76 ♥ QJ76 ♦ 54 ♣ K73

You are again 4-4 in the majors, with only 11 HCP, bid 1NT* to show 8-13 HCP and the majors.

(5) ♠ Q76 ♥ QJ ♦ AQJ1098 ♣ 1073

Bid 2♣*, you have 12 HCP and a long minor in diamonds; if asked about the alert, explain the bid as a long 6+ cards in a minor and 8+ HCP. To ask about the minor, opener now bids 2NT*, explained as an asking bid; more on the responses soon.

You have opened 1♣* and partner responds 1♥# (transfer to spades). What is your rebid?

1) ♠ AQ765 ♥ AQJ ♦ 54 ♣ K73

With 16 HCP and a minimal hand, bid 3♠ inviting game. Partner will bid game with 9 or 10 HCP.

2) ♠A ♥AKQ7652 ♦ AK ♣ AQJ

You have 27 HCP and 6+ hearts. Refuse the transfer and bid your own suit, bid 2♥. Subsequent bids will get you to slam in hearts or notrump.

3) ♠ 976 ♥ 7 ♦ AKJ2 ♣ AKQ75

You have 17 HCP and three spades, bid 4♠ showing no slam interest.

4) ♠ AQ7 ♥ AQ6 ♦ AJ2 ♣ KQ109

You have 22 HCP and three-card supports in spades, accept the transfer and bid 2♠. If partner next bids 3♣* (GCB), he is showing a five-card suit. The TAB of 3♠* is asking partner about the quality of his heart suit. If partner bids 4♣* showing no honors, bid 4♠.

The bid of 4♦* would show the king since you have the ace and queen. You would now bid 4NT to ask for keycards (RKCB). Again * = alert.

5) ♠ Q10 ♥ AQ108 ♦ KQ54 ♣ AKJ

You have a balanced hand with only two spades and 21 HCP; accept the transfer with two to an honor.

6) ♠A ♥AK ♦ AKQ10652 ♣ AJ10

You have a seven-card diamond suit and an unbalanced hand with 26 HCP, bid your diamond suit, 3♦. Subsequent bids should get you to slam.

You have opened 1♣* and partner responds 2♦# (transfer to hearts), what is your rebid?

1) ♠ AKQ1076 ♥ A ♦ KQ ♣ KQ76

You have 25 HCP, bid your own suit 2♠.

2) ♠ AJ ♥ AKQ1076 ♦ KQ6 ♣ AK

This hand has 26 HCP, accept the transfer by jumping in hearts to show length; if partner next bids 4♥, you would next bid 4NT (1430 RKCB).

3) ♠ AK765 ♥ A976 ♦ AK10 ♣ 2

This hand has 17 HCP, but is too good to bid 4♥; instead bid 2♥. With the right cards, slam is possible. If partner bids 3♣* (GCB) showing five hearts, you would next bid 3♥* (TAB). If partner next bids 4♥*, showing two top honors (KQ), bid 4NT to see if he has the A♣.

4) ♠ A7 ♥ AKQ874 ♦ AK ♣ AKQ

This hand has 29 HCP and six hearts, bid 2♥. Partner will bid 3♣*. Do not make a TAB, you have the AKQ of hearts, instead, bid 3♠* (SAB) in spades. If partner bids 4♣* showing no shortness, bid 6♥; if partner bids 4♦* (a singleton spade), bid 7♥.

5) ♠ 765 ♥ A ♦ A10982 ♣ AQJ7

You have only 15 HCP; you cannot accept the transfer, bid 3♦ to show your five-card suit.

Bid the following hands after 1♣*, making the appropriate positive responses and rebids.

(1)	Opener:	♠ AQ764 ♥ AQJ ♦ 54 ♣ K73
	Partner:	♠K5 ♥ 109876 ♦ AJ7 ♣ 108
(2)	Opener:	♠ Q10 ♥ AQ108 ♦ KQ54 ♣ AKJ
	Partner:	♠ A52 ♥ 10976 ♦ AJ ♣ 10865
(3)	Opener:	♠ AK4 ♥ J98 ♦ 765 ♣ AKJ2
	Partner:	♠ 10987 ♥ K2 ♦ AJ7 ♣ 9865
(4)	Opener:	♠ AKQ5 ♥ A9876 ♦ KQ10 ♣ 7
	Partner:	♠ 10987 ♥ K5 ♦ AJ4 ♣ J865
(5)	Opener:	♠ J53 ♥ A9876 ♦ AK2 ♣ A7
	Partner:	♠ K10987 ♥ 53 ♦ Q84 ♣ K104
(6)	Opener:	♠ J82 ♥ A98♦ AKJ3 ♣ QJ2
	Partner:	♠ KQ76 ♥ 7 ♦ Q984 ♣ K1074

(1) After the bid of 1♣*, partner bids 2♦#. Because partner has three hearts, the transfer is accepted. Opener now bids 2♥. With a fit in hearts, partner responds with the GCB bid 3♣* to show five hearts. Next, opener bids 3♥* (TAB). Partner has no honors and responds, 3♠*. Opener bids game and signs off in 4♥.

(2) After the bid of 1♣*, partner bids 1♠# as a transfer to notrump. Opener has a balanced hand with four hearts and bids 2NT. Responder now bids 3♣ (Stayman) and opener responds 3♥. Opener now bids game with no interest in slam.

(3) After the bid of 1♣*, partner bids 1♠# as a transfer to notrump. Opener bids 1NT. With a weak 8 HCP, pass. Do not bid Stayman.

(4) After the bid of 1♣*, partner bids 1♠# and opener bids 1NT. Partner next bids 2♣ (Stayman), and opener bids 2♠. Partner invites by bidding 3♠. Opener next cuebids 4♣ and partner cuebids 4♦. Opener bids 5♠.

(5) After the bid of 1♣*, partner bids 1♥# (transfer to spades) and opener bids 1♠ having three-card support. Next, partner bids 3♣# (GCB) to show five spades. Even though you have a minimal hand, bid 3♠* (TAB). With only one honor in spades, partner bids 4♦. Opener next bids 4♠.

(6) After the bid of 1♣*, partner bids 1♠# and opener bids 1NT. Now partner bids 2♣ (Stayman) and opener bids 2♦. Partner supports diamonds by bidding 3♦, opener next bids 4♦, and partner bids the 5♦ game.

Positive Responses to 1♣*- Another Option

Instead of making the acceptance bids of 1♠ and 1NT, one may "accept" by bidding 2♣* which becomes an asking bid when the opener has 20+ HCP. Using this approach, partner responds:

2♦	8-9 HCP with fit
2♥	9-10 HCP with fit
2♠	11-12 HCP with fit
2NT	13+ HCP with fit

After the bid of 2♦, one bids 3♣* instead of 2♥. Then, responder bids:

3♦	8-9 HCP with fit
3♥	9-10 HCP with fit
3♠	11-12 HCP with fit
3NT	13+ HCP with fit

With a minimal hand 16 - 19 HCP and a fit, one accepts the transfer and does not use the asking bid of two clubs. Without a fit, one may bid notrump with a balanced hand to show values or again bid an independent five-card suit.

Responses to 1♣*-1NT*, 1♣*- 2♣*, and 1♣*- 2NT*

1♣* - 1NT* (4-4 in the majors)

When opening 1♣*, it often happens that your partner is 4-4 in the majors with 8-13 HCP. Because it is desirable to play in a major suit contract with a fit, we have found this bid to be useful since you know whether or not you have a fit in the major with only a single bid; most other Precision systems require several bids.

With a fit and a minimal balanced hand (16+ HCP), invite game by bidding three of the major; partner becomes captain of the hand.

Without a fit in a major, opener next bids 2NT (forcing); this asks partner for a stopper in a minor. Bid your minor suit stopper, with two stoppers bid 3NT, and with none, bid your best major. The bids of 3♣ and 3♦ are natural showing a five-card minor.

Opener Rebids (after 1♣* - 1NT*) – Summary

2♣/2♦	16+ HCP, 5+ card suit and no major fit
2♥/2♠	shows 3-card support for the major with ruffing values
2NT	Forcing (16+ HCP) asking partner to bid minor suit stoppers
	Responder (Partner) Rebids
	Bid minor stopper suit (Qxx)
	Both minors stopped, bid 3NT
	None – Bid best major
3♣/3♦	16+ HCP, 6+ card suit and no major fit
3♥/3♠	Invitational to game in the major with fit (16+HCP)
3NT	16 + HCP and usually 2-cards support in major
4♥/4♠	Sign-off
4NT	Ask asking Blackwood

35

1♣* - 2♣*

After the bid of 1♣* (16+ HCP), as responder, you often have a long 6+ card minor with two of the top three honors and 8+ HCP, a hand that may play well in notrump if the strong opening bidder has three-card support for the minor. In the 2/1 Game Force System, it is similar to having partner open 1NT (14/15-17) and using minor suit transfers with super accepts. Opener may bid 2NT* which asks partner to bid his long minor suit. Opener will usually sign-off in 3NT with three-card support in the minor and one honor and a minimal hand.

With an unbalanced hand, he may bid game in the minor. Alternatively, after responder's minor suit bid, partner may accept the bid minor by bidding at the four-level (4♣*/4♦*) which are TAB with interest in a minor suit slam. With no honors in the minor, bid game in the minor. With one or two honors, bid the minor suit slam, and with three, one bids the grand slam in the minor.

With at least one four-card minor it is usually best to first ask about the minor without first showing your five-card major. With or without a minor card fit, you should next show your major at the three-level. With a double fit, game or slam in a major or minor is possible.

However, opener has several options. With a five-card major, he may choose not to bid 2NT but instead bid his five-card major (2♥/2♠). With two cards to an honor or three-card supports, partner must support the major at the three-levels and without support bids his minor. Opener is now the captain of the hand. After a major suit agreement, opener will use RKCB. The bids follow.

Opener Rebids (after 1♣* - 2♣*) – Summary

> 2♥/2♠   Shows a 5-card major suit
>
> **Responder Rebids**
> Raise major with support or bid minor

2NT	Asking partner for Minor (bid it - 3♣/3♦)

Responder Rebids

3NT	Sign-off
4♣*/4♦*	Trump Asking Bid
(TAB)	

Opener Responses to TAB

0	Bid Game in Minors
1-2	Bid Slam
3	Bid Grand Slam

3NT	No interest in slam or the minor
4NT	Blackwood Ace Asking

1♣* - 2NT*

When opener opens 1♣*, and partner responds 2NT* (14+ HCP), you know you are in the slam zone having 30+ HCP. In general, you cannot stop the bidding short of 4NT.

After the bid of 2NT*, partner bids 3♣*. This is not Stayman but the **Baron Convention** that asks partner to bid his four-card suits up-the-line. Remember, you are trying to find a 4-4 fit in a major suit or to play in notrump. Playing the Baron Convention, the bid of 3NT is used to show a club suit with 6+ clubs. The bids follow.

Opener Rebids (after 1♣* - 2NT*) – Summary

3♦/3♥/3♠	Natural bids
3♣*	Baron asking bid
	Responder Bids
	Bid 4-card suits up-the-line
	3NT show 6+clubs
4NT	Quantitative

BIDDING EXAMPLES

How would you bid each of the following hands?

(1)	Opener:	♠ AK765 ♥ A976 ♦ AK10 ♣ 2
	Partner:	♠ Q94 ♥ QJ ♦ Q987542 ♣ A
(2)	Opener:	♠ AJ7 ♥ A109 ♦ AK10 ♣ A987
	Partner:	♠ K986 ♥ QJ87 ♦ Q98 ♣ K5
(3)	Opener:	♠ AJ76 ♥ A109 ♦ AK10 ♣ 1098
	Partner:	♠ K954 ♥ QJ87 ♦ Q98 ♣ K5
(4)	Opener:	♠ AJ76 ♥ A109 ♦ AK10 ♣ A98
	Partner:	♠ KQ43 ♥ KQJ7 ♦ Q98 ♣ K5
(5)	Opener:	♠ KQ2 ♥ A7 ♦ AQ875 ♣ K98
	Partner:	♠ A76 ♥ KQJ9 ♦ K ♣ QJ1052
(6)	Opener:	♠ KJ10 53 ♥ AKJ ♦ QJ ♣ Q98
	Partner:	♠ A76 ♥ Q109 ♦ K98 ♣ AJ105

(1) After bidding 1♣*, partner bids 2♣# showing a long minor; checking on the minor, opener bids 2NT and partner bids 3♦. Even with a diamond fit, opener must show his five-card major by bidding 3♠. What next?

Showing spades at the three-level, partner now bids 3♠; given your great diamond fit, cuebid 4♥. Partner should next cuebid 5♣. And you would bid 6♦ but miss your spade slam.

Because opener has four diamonds and five spades, even with a diamond fit, it is better to bid 2♠ (showing at least four). Partner with only three spades will rebid his diamonds. You can rebid your spades and partner will bid 4♠. Using EKCB, bid 5♣ to show your singleton. Partner would next bid 5♦, showing no keycards excluding clubs and next bid 5♠. You would bid 6♠.

(2) After bidding 1♣*, partner responds 1NT* to show 4-4 in the majors and 8-13 HCP.

Without a fit, opener bids 2NT* asking for a stopper in a minor. Partner responds 3NT (both minors stopper). Opener then passes.

(3) After bidding 1♣*, partner bid 1NT*; having a minimal hand (16 HCP) and four-card spade suit, opener bids 4♠.

(4) After opening 1♣*, partner bids 2NT to show 14+ HCP. You must bid 3♣* (asking partner to bid four-card suits up-the-line). Partner bids 3♥* and without four hearts, opener bids 3♠. Partner with four spades, bids 4NT (RKCB). With four keycards, opener bids 5♣ showing one or four. Next, partner bids 5NT (specific kings), opener shows the diamond king and bids 6♦. Responder now bids 7♠.

(5) After bidding 1♣*, partner bids 2NT*. Opener shows his five-card diamond suit by bidding 3♦. With a singleton diamond, partner bids 3NT. Opener next bids 6NT.

(6) After bidding 1♣*, partner bids 2NT*. Opener next bids 3♠, his five-card suit. Partner next bids 4♠. Opener then bids 4NT, and with only one keycard, partner bids 5♣. Opener bids 5♠.

Responses to Unusual Positive Responses after 1♣*

1♣* - 3♣*/3♦* (8-13 HCP and 0-3 Controls)

When opener bids 1♣* and partner has a distributional hand with the pattern 4-4-4-1 showing a singleton, 8-13 HCP, and less than four controls, he bids 3♣* or 3♦* to show a black or red singleton, respectively. The bid shows at least game going values and the opener usually knows immediately where the contract should be played.

Holding the hand: ♠ AKQ54 ♥ KQ4 ♦ 456 ♣AK,

the auction goes:

Opener	Partner
1♣*	3♦*

Opener knows immediately that the partnership has a nine-card spade fit. Given your hand, you need to locate the singleton. To find the singleton after the bids of 3♣* or 3♦*, the next sequential suit is bid.

Partner's responses are:

After 3♣* (black singleton), opener asks by bidding 3♦ (next step ask): the responses are:

3♥*	shows a club singleton
3♠*	shows a spade singleton

After 3♦* (red singleton), opener asks by bidding 3♥* (next step ask): the responses are:

3♠*	shows a diamond singleton
3NT*	shows a heart singleton

Having located the singleton, one next bids the singleton suit to find out about partner's controls (aces and king) in his hand. The cuebid is called a Control Asking Bid (CAB) where an A=2 and K=1 control. To respond to the CAB, partner bids in steps; the first step shows 0-2 controls (one ace and two kings), the second step shows 3, 4, etc. An example of the bidding sequence follows.

Opener	Responder
1♣*	3♦* (red singleton)
3♥* (asking bid)	3NT* (heart singleton)
4♥* (CAB)	

Opener	Responder
1♣*	3♣* (black singleton)
3♦* (asking bid)	3♥* (club singleton)
4♣* (CAB)	

The CAB is most often used when opener has interest in slam; without slam interest and only game going values (16-17 HCP), opener will usually bid game in a major. Observe that one may also bid game in notrump when responder has a black singleton by bidding 3NT. If you want to play in notrump after the red singleton ask, you must allow partner to play the contract. It may be wrong sided. The bid of 4NT by opener is Blackwood since the partnership has not agreed upon a suit. The sequence of bids follow for easy reference.

Opener Rebids after 3♣*

3♦*	Where is the singleton?
	3♥ * club singleton
	3♠* spade singleton
3NT	to play
4♥/4♠	to play
4NT	Blackwood ace asking

After finding out about the singleton, opener may next make a cuebid of the singleton (4♣*/4♠*). The cuebid is the CAB

Partner's responses are:

1st step 0-2 (at most one ace or two kings)
2nd step 3 (ace and king)
3rd step 4 (two aces)

Opener Rebids after 3♦*

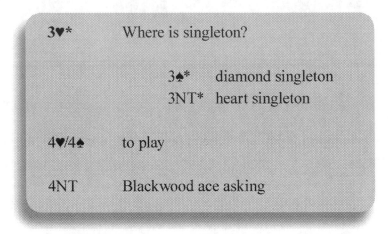

3♥*   Where is singleton?

             3♠*   diamond singleton
             3NT*   heart singleton

4♥/4♠   to play

4NT   Blackwood ace asking

After finding out about the singleton, opener may next make a cuebid of singleton (4♦*/4♥*). The cuebid is the CAB

Partner's responses are:

Step 1   0-2 (one ace or two kings)
Step 2   3 (ace and king)
Step 3   4 (two aces)

1♣* - 3♥*/3NT*/4♣*/4♦*   (14+ HCP and 4+Controls)

With more than 14+ HCP and a singleton (any 4-4-4-1 hand pattern) and 4+ controls, one makes submarine bids by bidding the suit directly below the singleton.

The submarine bids are:	3♥*	1=4=4=4	spade singleton
	3NT*	4=4=4=1	club singleton
	4♣*	4=4=1=4	diamond singleton
	4♦*	4=1=4=4	heart singleton

After opening 1♣*, these bids are in the slam zone. You cannot stop short of 4NT, the combined hands have 30 HCP and only 33 HCP are needed for a small slam. A grand slam requires 37 HCP.

After the strong unusual responses, the opener knows immediately the location of the singleton. To investigate slam, opener will use 4NT as Blackwood since the suit is unknown to partner (the responder). Keycard Blackwood (usually 1430) is used only if the suit of the contract is agreed upon.

The opening 1♣* bidder may also use Control Asking Bids to reach slam. **The bid is again a bid of the singleton (the next level bid).** However, now you are at a higher level and partner must have more than three controls.

The responses to the CAB (3♠*/4♣*/4♦*/4♥*) are:

Step 1	4 controls (two aces or ace and two kings)
Step 2	5 controls (two aces and one king/ace +three kings)
Step 3	6 controls (three aces/two aces and two kings) etc.

The above CAB step responses include the bid of 4NT.

Alternatively, opener may make natural bids with a minimal hand after the submarine bids:

Responder Bids		Natural Opener Rebids (16-17HCP)	
3♥*	1=4=4=4 spade singleton	3NT or 4♥	or 5♣/5♦
3NT*	4=4=4=1 club singleton	4♥/4♠	or 5♣/5♦
4♣*	4=4=1=4 diamond singleton	3NT or 4♥/4♠	or 5♣
4♦*	4=1=4=4 heart singleton	3NT or 4♠	or 5♣/5♦

After the opener makes a natural minimal major suit bid, partner knows the suit and will bid 4NT (RKCB) with slam interest.

1♣* - 3♠* solid 7+ card suit (AKQJxxx), 14 + HCP with or without side controls

When partner bids 3♠* over a 1♣* opening, it shows a solid suit equivalent to opening a Gambling 3NT if the suit is a minor or making the NAMYATS bids of 4♣* and 4♦*.

Opener Rebids (with minimal 16 – 17 HCP hand)

3NT	to play
4♥/4♠	natural showing at least 5-cards with no slam interest

Opener Rebids with 18+ HCP (if he knows the suit)

4♣*   CAB - Asks about outside suit controls

   Reponses to CAB bid are:

4♦*	no outside controls
4♥*	outside king
4♠*	outside ace or 2 kings
4NT*	ace/2-3 kings

Opener Rebids with 18 + HCP (if suit is unknown)

4♦*　　**asking for suit**

　　　　Responses to suit ask are:

　　　　4♥*/4♠*/5♣*　　hearts, spades, clubs
　　　　4NT*　　　　　　diamonds

Opener may also bid 4NT which is Blackwood only

BIDDING EXAMPLES

How would you bid each of the following hands after a 1♣* opening?

(1)	Opener:	♠ AK765 ♥ A976 ♦ AK10 ♣ 2
	Partner:	♠ QJ94 ♥ QJ108 ♦ Q987 ♣ A
(2)	Opener:	♠ AJ7 ♥ A109 ♦ AK10 ♣ A987
	Partner:	♠ K986 ♥ QJ87 ♦ Q ♣ K532
(3)	Opener:	♠ AJ76 ♥ AK10 ♦ AK10 ♣ A98
	Partner:	♠ K954 ♥ QJ97 ♦ Q987 ♣ K
(4)	Opener:	♠ AJ76 ♥ A109 ♦ AK10 ♣ K98
	Partner:	♠ KQ54 ♥ KQJ8 ♦ Q987 ♣ A
(5)	Opener:	♠ KQ2 ♥ A7 ♦ AQ875 ♣ K98
	Partner:	♠ A763 ♥ KQJ9 ♦ K ♣ QJ105
(6)	Opener:	♠ A10986 ♥ 7 ♦ AQ ♣ AKQ98
	Partner:	♠ 7 ♥ AKQJ865 ♦ K7 ♣ J76

(1) After bidding 1♣*, partner with 4=4=4=1 distribution, 12 HCP and one control bids 3♣* to show a black suit singleton. The opener knows immediately that the partnership has a 4-4 card heart fit. With 18 HCP, partner next bids 3♦* (where is your singleton?); partner bids 3♥* to show the club singleton. Now, opener knows that the partnership is 5-4 in spades

and 4-4 in hearts. Partner invites slam by bidding 5♥. Because partner has the A♣, he bids 6♥. It is only a 30 HCP slam but a great contract.

(2) After bidding 1♣*, partner with 4=4=1=4 distribution, 11 HCP and two controls bids 3♦* to show a red singleton. The opener knows immediately that the partnership is 4-3 in the majors. With 20 HCP and two stoppers in diamonds, one in hearts, and a balanced hand, opener bids 3NT showing no slam interest.

(3) After bidding 1♣*, partner with 4=4=1=4 distribution, 11 HCP and two controls bids 3♣* to show a black singleton. With 20 HCP, partner next bids 3♦* (where is your singleton?); partner next bids 3♥* to show the club singleton. Now, opener knows that the partnership has a 4-4 spade fit. Partner bids 4NT (Blackwood) and then 5NT. Hearing the response 5♥, showing two kings, even with all the aces and king because of the known club singleton, opener bids 6♠.

(4) After bidding 1♣*, partner with 4=4=4=1 distribution, 14 HCP and four controls makes the submarine bid of 3NT* to show a club singleton. With 22 HCP, partner next bids 4♣* (CAB). With an ace and two kings, partner bids 4♦* (one step). Opener bids 6♠/6NT.

(5) After bidding 1♣*, partner with 4=4=1=4 distribution, 19 HCP and six controls makes the submarine bid of 4♣* to show a diamond singleton. With 18 HCP, partner next bids 4♦* (CAB). With an ace and two kings, partner bids 4♥* (one step). Opener bids 6 NT.

(6) After bidding 1♣*, partner with a long heart suit and 14 HCP bids 3♠*. Opener with a singleton heart knows that the suit is hearts. Opener bids 4♣* asking about outside controls; with and outside king, partner bids 4♦. Opener next bids 7NT.

Chapter 4 - Responding to 1♣* with Interference

WHEN PLAYING PRECISION, EXPECT the opponents to interfere. Everyone wants to compete over the 1♣* opening; after all, it is only at the one-level. Partnerships need specific agreements to cope with interference.

Interference comes in many flavors. There are natural bids, artificial bids, and two-suited bids among others that are designed to interfere in the direct or balancing seat. As a Precision player, you must be prepared for all situations. Before discussing how to cope with interference in both the direct and balancing seats, we review a few systems partnerships may use to interfere with Precision.

Overview of Interference Systems used over Precision 1♣*

Mathe

The most popular system is called Mathe, developed by Lewis L. Mathe from California. It is popular because of its simplicity. It goes:

> Over 1♣*, bids in the direct seat are:
>
> Double*   4-4 or better in the majors
> 1NT*   4-4 or better in the minors
> 2NT*   5-5 or better in the minors

All one-level bids are natural (diamonds, hearts, and spades) and the bid of 2♣ shows a club suit. The system is also used in the balancing seat over the sequence: 1♣* - Pass - 1♦* - (?)

Because both bids are artificial, all Mathe responses remain the same; however, now two clubs and two diamonds are natural. Higher two-level bids usually show a distributional hand. A disadvantage of Mathe is that the double does not interfere significantly over the strong club bid. An alternate is the system Bill Amason and I call SPAM, which says **SP**ades **A**nd **M**ore, to be used against other Precision players.

SPAM (played in the direct seat only)

The bids follow.

Double	the majors (4-4 or 5-4)
1♠*	takeout with an unspecified long suit 5+ cards
1NT*	the minors (5-5)
2♣*	the majors (5-5)
2♦*	diamonds and a major (5-5)
2NT*	strong notrump 15-17 HCP
3X	Natural suit 6+ cards

CRASH

Another convention used by some partnerships is called CRASH, representing **C**olor **RA**nk and **SH**ape. The system was developed by Kit Woolsey and Steve Robinson. The basic bids are:

Double*	2 suits of the same color (red or black)
1♦*	2 suits of the same rank (majors or minors)
1NT*	2 suits of the same shape (rounded ♣ ♥ or pointed ♦ ♠)
1♥/1♠/2♣/2♦	shows natural 5+ card suits

CRASH, like Mathe, may also be employed in the balancing seat.

Mathe and CRASH are probably the most widely used systems to interfere over the Precision club. Because many 2/1 Game Force partnerships play some version of DONT or Weber (Transfer bids), I have modified the bids to make them consistent with Modified DONT (Meckwell). The system is similar to DONT+T (ON), developed by Tony Melucci in cooperation with Neill Currie. The bids follow. I call the system MDONT +T.

MDONT + T (played in the direct seat only)

1♦*	Transfer to hearts with 5+ hearts
1♥*	Transfer to spades with 5+ spades
1♠*	Transfer to clubs
1NT*	Transfer to diamonds
2♣*	Clubs + Major
2♦*	Diamonds + Major
2♥*	Hearts + Spades (the majors are at least 4-4)
2NT*	Clubs + Diamond (the minors are at least 5-5)

Higher level bids are natural.

Another system developed by Tony Melucci and Neill Currie is called MACE. Because some feel that coping with the MACE bids is difficult, I have included their system of bids.

MACE

Double*	4-4 in the Minors
1♦*	shows 3-3 or 4-3 in the Majors
1♥/1♠	Natural 5+ card suit
1NT*	Rounded or Points Suits (4-4 or better)
2NT*	Both Majors or Both Minors (5-5 or better)

Suit bids at the two- or three-levels are natural

When should you interfere over Precision and what is the best system?

The guidelines for interference over the strong club follow those you used when playing 2/1 Game Force. In the direct seat, you need a distributional hand and in the balancing seat you need shortness. Again, the rules of 8 and 2 apply.

Rule of 2

You should interfere over the bid of 1♣* in the balancing seat if you have at least two shortness points. Otherwise, do not interfere.

Rule of 8

Provided you have at least 6 HCP, you should interfere over 1♣* in the direct seat if the number of cards in your two longest suits minus the number of losers in your hand is two or more. Otherwise, do not interfere.

The best system to play over Precision is the one you remember. The simplest are SPAM and Mathe. Even though MDONT +T addresses the most hand combinations, SPAM is simple and provides adequate interference over the strong club opening; more importantly, it is easily remembered.

General Approach with interference

When the opponents interfere, you should always use your established understandings. For example, over a double, all bids are per the Precision System of bids you would normally use; ignore the double.

Another common practice is to use "Stolen Bids." For example, if the opponents bid 1♠ for takeout, the double means they stole your bid, hence it is a transfer to 1NT and all other bids are natural; similarly, if 1♥ is natural, then double is a transfer to spades, and 2♦ is a transfer to hearts. If one cannot make your agreed upon "system bids," then specific understandings must be agreed upon.

We do not recommend stolen bids but assume all bids are natural and that a double shows 5-7 HCP. We next consider several specific situations.

Coping with Interference in the Direct Seat

Double (no meaning)

Because many players do not have a system they play over 1♣*, it often only implies an opening hand. Then, bid:

Pass   0-4 HCP
1♦   5-7

You should always ignore the double and just make your standard bids (e.g., 1♥, 1♠, 2♦, 2♣, 1NT, 2NT, etc.).

Double (shows majors)

Over Mathe, a system that shows the majors, one uses the following bids.

Pass	0-4 HCP
Redouble	5-7 HCP
1♥	8-10 HCP no stopper in hearts
1♠	8-10 HCP no stopper in spades
1NT	8-10 HCP stoppers in the majors
2♣	8-13 HCP and 6+ cards
2♦	8-13 HCP and 6+ diamonds
2♥	11+ spade stopper (no heart stopper)
2♠	11+ heart stopper (no heart stopper)
2NT	11+ both majors stopped

Natural one-level bids or strong NT

When playing against Precision, many pairs use natural bids for example 1♦, 1♥, 1♠, and 2♣, showing diamonds, hearts, spades, and clubs. The following bidding structure is recommended.

If the bid is a natural suit bid at the one-level, then one bids:

Pass	0-4 HCP
Double	5-7 HCP
Suit	8+ HCP, 5+ card suit, Game Force
Jump in suit	10+ HCP, 5/6+ suits, Game Force
1NT	8-13 HCP, with stopper
2NT	10+ HCP, with 1/2 stopper
Cuebid	14+ HCP, Game Force no stopper

If the bid of 1NT is strong 15 -17 HCP, then one bids:

Pass	0-4 HCP
Double	5-7 HCP
Suit	8+ HCP, 5+ card suit

What if the bid of 1NT is Mathe? Now, the bid shows the minors. Similar to playing 2/1 Game Force, one may make "unusual over unusual" type cuebids and natural bids. The structure for the bids follow.

Pass	0-4 HCP
Redouble	5-7 HCP
2♣	5+ hearts, GF
2♦	5+ spades GF
2♥	5+ HCP, natural and non-forcing
2♠	5+ HCP, natural and non-forcing
3NT	10+ HCP, both minors stopped

Two-suited hands (not the majors)

When the two suits are known, one may again employ cuebids and natural bids. For example, suppose the overcall of a diamond shows diamonds and hearts. Then a cuebid of the lower ranking suit would show 5+ clubs and a cuebid of the higher ranking suit would show 5+ spades. Again, one would pass with 0-4 HCP and a double show 5-7 HCP and may be left in for penalty.

Two-, Three-, and Four-level overcalls

Interference by the opponents at the two-level or higher cause significant problems; however, a double is always used to show 5-7 HCP. Recommended bidding structures follow.

At 2-level – (natural)

Pass	0-4 HCP
Double	5-7 HCP
Suit bid	8+ HCP, natural
2NT	11-13 HCP with stopper
3NT	14+ with stoppers

At 3-level – (natural)

Pass	0-4 HCP
Double	4-7 HCP
Suit bid	8+ HCP, and 5+ card suit

At 4-level – (natural)

Pass	0-4 HCP
Double	5-7 HCP, takeout or penalty

BIDDING EXAMPLE

How would you bid each of the following hands after a 1♣* and the opponents interfere?

(a) 1♠* takeout
(b) Double – the majors
(c) 1NT* the minors
(d) 2♣ natural
(e) 2♦* diamonds and hearts

And you hold the following hand: (1) ♠ K986 ♥ QJ87 ♦ Q98 ♣ K5

(1a) With 11 HCP and a stopper in spades, double as a transfer to 1NT.
(1b) With both majors stopped bid 1NT naturally.
(1c) Cuebid 2♣ to show hearts, partner may support hearts or bid spades.
(1d) Double for takeout.

(1e) Bid 3NT showing stoppers.

Coping with Interference in the Balancing Seat

The bidding has gone 1♣* - Pass - 1♦* and the opponents, knowing your partner is weak showing 0-7 HCP, may enter the auction. The most common bids in this situation is for your RHO to bid a major or use Mathe in the balancing seat where 1NT shows the minors and a double is for both majors. Example bidding schemes for several situations follow.

After 1♣* - (Pass) - 1♦* - (1♥/♠)

Pass	balanced minimum no 5-card suit
Double	support for the other 3 suits
Suit Bid	Natural, non-forcing
1NT	shows stopper with (16-21 HCP)
2NT	shows stopper with (22+ HCP)
Cuebid	20 + HCP no stopper

After 1♣* - (Pass) - 1♦* - (1NT for Minors)

Pass	balanced minimum no 5-card suit
Double	support for the both majors
2♣/2♦	unusual cuebids and extra values with ♥/♠
2♥/2♠	Natural non-forcing
2NT	shows stopper with (22+ HCP)

After 1♣* - (Pass) - 1♦* - (Double = Majors)

Pass	balanced minimum no 5-card suit
Double	support for the both minors
2♣/2♦	natural 5+ card suit.
2♥/2♠	unusual cuebids shows extra values and ♣/♦
2NT	shows stopper with (22+ HCP)

Chapter 5 – Preemptive Responses to 1♣*

To show a weak major suit hand, one bids of 2♥/2♠. The bids show a weak major suit hand with 6+ cards and only 4-6 HCP. A summary of the bids follow.

<table>
<tr><td colspan="3">Opener Rebids</td></tr>
<tr><td>Pass</td><td colspan="2">Game unlikely</td></tr>
<tr><td>4♥/4♠/3NT</td><td colspan="2">20+ HCP</td></tr>
<tr><td>New suit</td><td colspan="2">5+ cards without support for the majors</td></tr>
<tr><td></td><td colspan="2">Partner's Rebids</td></tr>
<tr><td></td><td>Raise</td><td>3+ support (or Qx)</td></tr>
<tr><td></td><td>Rebid ♥/♠</td><td>min no support</td></tr>
<tr><td></td><td>Cuebid under 3NT</td><td>singleton or void</td></tr>
<tr><td>3♥/3♠</td><td colspan="2">Minimal hand with support (16-18 HCP)</td></tr>
<tr><td></td><td colspan="2">Partner's Rebids</td></tr>
<tr><td></td><td colspan="2">Pass or bid game</td></tr>
<tr><td>2NT</td><td colspan="2">Ogust</td></tr>
<tr><td>3NT</td><td colspan="2">Natural</td></tr>
<tr><td>4NT</td><td colspan="2">RKCB</td></tr>
</table>

If instead of making a weak jump shift at the two-level, but bidding 3♥/3♠, the bid is again very weak showing 7+ cards in the bid suit.

> Let's look at an example hand.
>
> Opener: ♠ KQ987 ♥ 109 ♦ AK3 ♣ AQJ
>
> Partner: ♠ J5   ♥ KQ9875 ♦ 542 ♣ 87

After the bid of 1♣* by opener, partner now bids 2♥ to show 4-6 HCP and six hearts. With only two hearts, opener must pass.

For each of the following hands, suppose you open 1♣* and partner responds two spades. What is your rebid?

> (1)   ♠ 7 ♥ AQ756 ♦ AQ2 ♣ AKQJ
>
> (2)   ♠ AK97 ♥ J5 ♦ AQ10 ♣ AJ98
>
> (3)   ♠ 7 ♥ AQ10985 ♦ AK ♣ KJ74

(1) With 22 HCP, bid 3NT.
(2) With 19 HCP, bid 4♠.
(3) With a minimal hand and no fit, pass.

You should respond at the three-level after partner opens one club if you have a hand like the following.

♠ 72 ♥ KJ109852 ♦ 7 ♣ 654 bid 3♥.

Chapter 6 – Major Suit Openings

Playing the 2/1 Game Force System, the bid of a major suit shows 12-21 starting points that includes HCP and length. However, playing Precision, it shows 11-15 HCP and a five-card suit. You know immediately that opener's hand is limited.

When responding to a major suit opening, remember that 25-26 points will usually produce a major suit game. When partner opens a major, partner has at least 11 HCP and two quick tricks. With a fit (3+ cards) and upon reevaluation of your hand if you have 13+ **Dummy Points,** you have game in a major. Some may argue you need 14+ HCP, but this is not the case since playing 2/1, the opening bidder has 12+ HCP that includes one length point or only 11 HCP as in Precision.

A game forcing response by responder is accomplished by showing a new suit at the two-level without jumping or skipping a bidding level. After a major suit opening, and the OPPONENTS HAVE PASSED and YOU ARE NOT A PASSED HAND, game force bids are:

Opening bid	Game Forcing Responses
1♠	2♣/2♦ (4+cards), 2♥ (5+cards)
1♥	2♣/ 2♦ (4+cards)

The game forcing bid is always made in a suit that has at least four-cards and is **forcing** for one round of bidding. The opener may not pass (unless the opponents interfere); the pass made by the opener is called a forcing pass since your side has established a game force bidding sequence.

The only real difference between Precision bids and the bids you used playing the 2/1 Game Force System is there is no such thing as a reverse and strong jump shifts. If you make a reverse playing Precision it shows shape since opener has no more than 15 HCP. The bid of 1NT is semi-forcing, Concealed/Ambiguous splinters, Jacoby 2NT, and Swiss bids all apply. Playing Combined Bergen Raises, the bids in Precision and 2/1 are identical. A review of the bids follow.

If one opens a major and responder has four-card support, and between 5-12 Dummy Points, one may use Bergen Raises to show the nature of the support.

Bergen and Combined Bergen Raises

Suppose partner opens 1♥/1♠ and you have **four-cards support,** one bids:

3♣* shows 7-9 Dummy Points with 4-card support

3♦* shows 10-12 Dummy Points with 4-card support (called a limit raise)

If one reverses these two bids, the two bids are called Reverse Bergen Raises.

Because these bids are made at the three-levels, they may be played when the opponents interfere with a double. They are free bids; however, many pairs play that Bergen Raises are off. Others have devised a special system called BROMAD (Bergen Raise over Major Suit Double). A disadvantage of the BROMAD Convention is that it eliminates several standard bids. I do not recommend it.

However, some play that over interference the bids do not apply and are always off. I believe that this is too extreme. Why do you allow the opponents to interfere with your bidding sequences? I recommend they be played over two-level bids when they may be made, vulnerable or non-vulnerable.

For example, if the bidding goes 1♠ - 2♥ - there is room for the three-level bids always. If the overcall is a minor suit bid of say 2♣, then 3♣ (a cuebid) only ensures at least 3+ card support for the major suit bid of 1♠, even though you may have four. **Finally, they are always on over a double!**

Another system that has become popular is called "Combined Bergen" Raises, developed by Pat Peterson from Hernando, Florida. I like the convention. It works like this.

3♣* shows 7-12 Dummy Points (note that we have combined the Bergen point range for this bid; hence the name Combined Bergen) with four-card support, if opener wants to know whether or not you are at the lower end (7-9) points, or higher end (10-12) points, opener bids 3♦*. The response 3♥* shows the lower range and the response 3♠* shows the upper range.

3♦* shows 10-12 Dummy Points with three-card support (a limit raise)

Thus, you do not have to bid 1NT (semi-forcing) and make a jump rebid in the major with 10-12 Dummy Points. One normally has 0-2 card trump support for the bid major. The schedule for Combined Bergen bids follows.

Combined Bergen Raises with Interference
Max Hardy Swiss Bids and Concealed/Ambiguous Splinters

Dummy Pts	No Interference	Double	Suit bid	Passed Hand
	2 Trumps			
5-9 Pts	*1NT then 2 Major	pass	pass	pass
	3 Trumps			
5-9 Pts	*1NT then 2 Major	pass	pass	pass
8-10(bad) Pts	@2 Major (Const.)	2 Major	2 Major	2 Major
10-12 Pts	@3♦**	Redouble	Cuebid	Drury (2♣*)
13+	2 over 1 Bids	Redouble	Cuebid	N/A
16+ Pts Balanced	@4♣ (Swiss)	@4♣	@4♣	N/A
	4 Trumps			
0-6 Pts	@3 Major (Weak)	@3 Major	@3 Major	@3 Major
7-12 Pts	@3♣**	@3 Clubs	2 Major	2 Major
	Bid 3 Diamonds to			
	Ask 3♥=7-9, 3♠=10-12			
13+ Singleton	@3 Other Major	@3 Other Major	@3 Other Major	N/A
(Concealed Splinter)	then Step Bids#			
13+ No Singleton	2 over 1 Bid	2 over 1 Bid	2 over 1 Bid	N/A
15/16+ Pts	@Jacoby 2NT	@Jacoby 2NT	@Jacoby 2NT	N/A
	5 Trumps			
0-11 Pts	Bid Game	Bid Game	Bid Game	Bid Game
12-15 Pts	@4♦ (Swiss)	@4♦	@4♦	N/A

Note: With 5 HCP and three-card trump support, pass unless holding either a singleton or at least one trump honor with all other HCP in one side suit. *Semi-Forcing **=Forcing, @=Alert

after 3♠ bid 3NT to find singleton/void, then 4♣/4♦/4♥/4♠ denote Singleton/void. After 3♥, bid 3♠, again steps denote the singleton. For example, 3NT denotes club singleton/void, etc. If you want to know if it is a singleton/void, bid next suit up which are Scroll Bids.

The above table also applies to Bergen Raises, one only need change the bid of 3♣** to show 7-9 points with four-card support and 3♦** to show four-card support with 10-12 points, 1NT* followed by three of the major to show 10-12 points with three-card support and Jacoby 2NT requires only 13+ starting points and four-card support.

If the overcall is at the two-level, we also use the Bergen bids; however, if the bid is, for example, 2♣, the bid of 3♣* may show three- or four-card support because of its cuebid nature.

Truscott Jordan 2NT

In the Combined Bergen Convention, we have chosen not to include the Truscott Jordan 2NT bid. If used, it is not the same as the Jacoby 2NT bid. The bid is typically used to show a limit raise with three- or four-card support for the bid of a major over a double (it must be alerted). We recommend the Redouble which shows 10+ points with or without a fit. After a redouble, one next supports the major (shows 13+ with three- or four-card support for the major). If you redouble and bid your own suit, you are denying a fit. Discuss these options with your partner.

We recommend the Jordan 2NT over a minor suit opening if you do not play Flip-Flop. It shows 5+ card support and a limit raise. Recall that playing Flip-Flop, 2NT is weak and a three-level bid of the minor shows a limit raise.

Chapter 7 – Opening 1NT

As we stated in the introduction, the opening bid of 1NT shows 13-15 HCP and a balanced hand (4-3-3-3, 4-4-3-2, or 5-4-4-2). The bid is neither really weak nor strong; however, when responding to the bids playing Precision, it is closer to "weak" notrump bids than strong 15-17 bids played in the 2/1 Game Force System.

Responder with a balanced hand must take into account that game is possible only if he has a minimum of 12 HCP and opener has a maximum hand. Hence, with a balanced hand, no five-card suit and fewer than 12 HCP, responder must pass. Responder does not use transfer bids after the opening bid of 1NT. Two hearts and two spades are to play. Three-level bids are invitational. We review the bids after opening 1NT.

2♣/2♦ non-forcing (10-12 HCP) /forcing Stayman (12+ HCP) and only used if not a passed hand. The bid of 2♦ by a passed hand is to play.

Other bids follow.

2♣	NF Stayman	10-12 HCP
2♦	Forcing Stayman	13+ HCP
2♥/2♠	to PLAY	0-8 HCP
3♣/3♦/3♥/3♠	6-card suit with 2 of top 3 honors	9-11 HCP

After Stayman, opener bids 2♦/2NT with no four-card major, two of a major with four, where 2♥ may imply both.

After 1NT-2♣-2♦

Pass	Drop Dead Stayman with 4-4-4-1
2♥	Garbage Stayman (pick best 3-card major)
2NT	invitational
3m	5+ card suits, game forcing, slam oriented. By a passed hand it is invitational with a 4-card major and 5+ cards in the minor.
3M	Smolen
4♣	Gerber
4♦, 4♥	Delayed Texas transfer, 6+ 4 in the majors, no slam interest/very strong hand with a void
4NT, 5NT	Quantitative
5M	GSF

After 1NT-2♣-2M:

2NT	invitational
3m	5+ card suits, game forcing, slam oriented. By a passed hand it is invitational with a 4-card major and 5+ cards in the minor.
3M	Invitational
Sets M as trump suit, and responder may be planning to RKCB in M in his next bid (kickback/1430).	
4m	void, fit in M, slam interest.
4NT, 5NT	Quantitative
5M	GSF
5m	Signoff

Interference with weak NT is common. After a double, 1NT-double, the following scheme may be used.

Modified DONT (Meckwell) Notrump Runouts

Meckwell Runouts bids are similar to the notrump overcall convention; hence, they share the same name. Playing this convention, after the auction has begun 1NT-Double (for penalty), a Redouble shows a single-suited hand and forces partner to bid 2♣ so that you can pass or correct to your suit.

All bids at the two-level show a two-suited hand with the bid suit and a higher-ranking suit: 2♣ shows clubs and a major suit, 2♦ shows diamonds and a major, 2♥ shows both majors, and 2NT shows the minors. All three-level bids show a long suit and are to play and Texas transfers are on. If you have a good hand and want to play 1NT doubled, you should pass. For the purposes of runout bids, a hand is two-suited if it is 4-4 or better, and it is single-suited if it contains a six-card or longer suit or a five-card suit without another four-card suit. If 4-3-3-3, it is usually best to pretend the hand is two-suited.

BIDDING EXAMPLES

How would you bid each of the following hands after a 1NT opening?

> **(1) ♠ Q5 ♥ J75 ♦ KQ8762 ♣ Q5**

You have 10 HCP, bid 3♦

> **(2) ♠ A7 ♥ KQJ987 ♦ AQ53 ♣ 7**

You have 16 HCP, bid 2♦ and jump in hearts (3♥) to show six-card suit.

> **(3) ♠ Q765 ♥ J964 ♦ 987 ♣ J7**

Bid 2♣, if opener bids a major, pass. If opener bids 2♦, bid 2♥ (Garbage Stayman), pick best three-card suit.

> **(4) ♠ Q764 ♥ A942 ♦ AQ2 ♣ J4**

Bid 2♣, if partner bids 2♠, invite by bidding 3♠. After a rebid of 2♦, bid 2NT.

(5) ♠ A62 ♥ AQ10 ♦ A873 ♣ J42

Bid 3NT.

(6) ♠ Q65 ♥ KQ7 ♦ AKJ52 ♣ 74

You have 15 HCP; bid 2♦ game forcing and then 3NT. Suppose instead of 15 HCP, you only had 10-12 HCP; now you would bid 2♣, and after a bid of a major by opener bid 3♦, a non-forcing sequence of bids.

Bidding by a Passed Hand (Double barreled Stayman off)

Now, 2♣ is the Stayman and 2♦ is a transfer to hearts; however, all invitational three-level bids are appropriate.

What would the sequence   1NT - 2♣;
                       2♦ - 3♥; or 2♠ - 3♥;

mean? This delayed three-level bid shows a six-card suit but would suggest game in notrump or hearts, respectively. For example, suppose you had the following hand:

♠ 65 ♥ AQJ752 ♦ K53 ♣ 109

As opener, you would pass, but if partner bids 1NT, you would use the above sequence of bids. With five hearts, you would now bid 2♦ as a transfer.

COMPLETE BIDDING SEQUENCES over 1NT Opening

(1)　♠ Q98　　♠ KJ742　　(2)　♠ A743　　♠ Q1094
　　♥ A76　　♥ K5　　　　　♥ A92　　♥ QJ75
　　♦ AK56　♦ Q842　　　　♦ A7　　　♦ Q54
　　♣ Q73　　♣ 54　　　　　♣ 9643　　♣72

1NT　　　　2♥ (to play)　　1NT　　　　2♣ (Stayman)
3♦ (forcing)　4♥　　　　　2♥　　　　pass

(3)　♠ KQ873　♠ J6　　　(4)　♠ KJ43　　♠ A1094
　　♥ KQ4　　♥ AJ10　　　　♥ J92　　♥ A2
　　♦ 562　　♦ 7　　　　　♦ K75　　♦ AQ9654
　　♣ K8　　♣ AQ76542　　♣ AK5　　♣7

1NT　　　　3♦ (9-11 HCP)　1NT　　　　2♦ (Stayman)
3♠ (forcing)　4♥　　　　　2♠　　　　3♠
5♣　　　　pass　　　　　　4♣　　　　4♦
4♠　　　　5♠
6♠

Chapter 8 – Weak Two Major and Preemptive Bids

Weak Two Bids

WEAK MAJOR SUIT OPENINGS of 2♠/2♥ will be played as in 2/1 Game Force. The bids show a six-card suit with 5-10 HCP. The bids ensure at least one of the top three honors. Occasionally, when non-vulnerable you may have only a five-card suit. The object of the bid is to interfere with the opponents' bidding.

Rule of 17

When responding to a major suit two-level opening bid, one may use the RULE OF 17. The rule goes as follows. If the number of Dummy Points and the number of cards in the major suit bid total 17, bid to the four-level in the major.

With 12-15 Dummy Points and two-card support, raise the two-level bid to three; a weak competitive raise is non-forcing and need not be alerted. It is called by some "raise only non-forcing" (RONF). Any new suit by responder is also non-forcing but must be alerted. With 15-16 starting points, responder makes a forcing 2NT bid, which asks the opening bidder to describe his hand and is invitational to game in the major with at least two-card support or notrump, independent of vulnerability.

The OGUST Convention

After a weak two bid (usually a six-card suit), the convention allows for a detailed description of the opener's hand. It is invoked by the artificial 2NT bid made by the responder. The reply to a weak two bid shows strength and asks whether the opener is weak (5-7/6-8 starting points) or strong (8-10/9-11 starting points) and how many of the top three honors are held in the major. The replies are most commonly as follows.

3♣	minimum, 1 top suit honor (BAD/WEAK Hand and BAD/STRONG Suit)
3♦	minimum, 2 top suit honors (BAD/WEAK Hand and GOOD/STRONG Suit)
3♥	maximum, 1 top suit honor (GOOD/ STRONG Hand and BAD/WEAK Suit)
3♠	maximum, 2 top suit honors (GOOD/ STRONG Hand and GOOD/STRONG Suit)
3NT	all 3 honors, A-K-Q-x-x-x and little else

A simple way to remember this is to picture Mamma Mia dancing. 1-2, 1-2, 1-2-3... These refer to the order of the top honors in the major as shown above. The bids represent HAND and then SUIT - **NOT SUIT and then HAND!**

NOTE: Some players interchange the bids of three diamonds and three hearts. The 1-1, 2-2, 1-2-3 dance step!

Some players incorrectly use the convention to show first suit and not hand. Discuss

this convention with your partner. The word OGUST may have a different meaning to your partner! This is why a description of any convention is better than using simply the words "I play Ogust." The OGUST Convention is used instead of "asking" for a feature (ace or king).

What if responder has his own suit? We have said that a raise in opener's suit is non-forcing. When partner bids his own suit, it is most often played as forcing for one round and asks partner to support the suit bid with three-card support or to pass. If you do not play it as forcing, you must alert the new bid as non-forcing "it appears in red on your convention card."

Modified OGUST Convention

Because bidding is becoming more aggressive, many partnerships will open weak twos with a five-card major one suiter. If you do, one may use Modified OGUST rebids to describe the hand. Again, the 2NT bid is used to ask about the hand. Using this convention, the bids are:

3♣	5-card suit GOOD/STRONG hand
3♦	5-card suit BAD/WEAK hand
3♥	6-card suit BAD/WEAK hand
3♠	6-card suit GOOD/STRONG hand

3NT   either a 5- or 6-card suit or a semi-solid 5- or 6-card suit plus ace or king in a side suit

Observe that the 3♣ bid is used to show a stronger HAND in order to leave more room for further investigation since all responses describe only the **"HAND"** and say nothing about the quality of the suit.

If after the response of the 3♣ bid, responder wants to find out about the **SUIT,** one bids 3♦*. The opener now clarifies the suit strength with the following bids.

3♥*	BAD/WEAK suit and 1 honor
3♠*	GOOD/STRONG suit and 2 honors
3NT*	GOOD/STRONG suit and 3 honors

Following OGUST, one describes the HAND and upon request, then the SUIT.

A common practice is to use five-card OGUST Non-Vulnerable and six-card OGUST Vulnerable!

If you do not make this distinction (five- and six-cards) in your partnership agreement, there is yet another convention called the TWO-STEP OGUST Convention developed by Daniel Zenko. It is discussed in the April 1997 issue of "The Bridge World."

While experts use OGUST type responses for two-suited 6-4 hands in the majors, the responses become complicated and will not be discussed.

Opening three- and four-level bids

Opening bids at the three-level are preemptive showing a weak hand (5-10 HCP) and are able to take about five tricks in the trump suit bid. To open the bidding one usually has a seven-card suit and no ace or king in an outside suit or four cards in a major. Vulnerable you should hold two of the top three honors in the suit bid. **Once you make a three-level bid, you have described your entire hand, so do not bid again, unless partner makes a forcing bid.** The only ways partner can force is by bidding a new suit, by cuebidding the opponent's suit, or by asking for aces. Or, if you play 3NT* as Ogust at the three-level, it is forcing.

Opening at the four-level is also preemptive showing a weak hand; one is usually able to take six tricks in the trump suit. Now, you need an eight-card suit, no outside ace or king, no four card major, and three of the top five honors. You only get one bid.

Rule of 2/3

A guide to preemptive opening bids and overcalls is that one cannot afford to be set more than 500 unless one is saving against a slam contract. One often assumes that a vulnerable partner can make two tricks, and a non-vulnerable partner three tricks. Thus, a player who opens 4♠ should have an eight playing trick hand if vulnerable, and a seven playing trick hand if not vulnerable. **To count playing tricks, only the first three tricks in a suit are counted. Winners are the A, K, or Q only in the suit.** With less than three cards, there are these loser honor exceptions: AQ = ½, Kx = ½, KQ = 1, K = 1, Q=1, Qx=2.

What does that mean? The Rule of 2/3 states that with a weak hand and a long, strong suit, you should count your playing tricks and add three when non-vulnerable, and add two if vulnerable.

To illustrate, we consider two hands:

A) ♠AKQ10653 ♥ 8 ♦ 954 ♣ 96   B) ♠ void ♥ 63 ♦ AQJ876432 ♣ 87

In Hand A, you have six losers (0 in spades, 1 in hearts, 3 in diamonds, and 2 in clubs). 13 cards-6 losers=7 **playing tricks**. Non-vulnerable, adding 3, 7+3=10 so you should open 4♠. If you open at only the three-levels, you would be underbidding your cards. You would open 3♠ only if vulnerable (7+2=9).

In Hand B, you have five losers. 13-5= 8 playing tricks. Non-vulnerable, adding 3, 8+3 + 11 so you would open five diamonds. If vulnerable, bid only four diamonds.

Opening 3NT* Gambling

To use the bid of Gambling 3NT*, you must have a solid running minor suit with 7+ cards with the AKQ and usually the J. However, when it comes to strength outside the minor suit, not all agree upon the requirements. The bid is always alerted.

In the first seat, most play the bid with no values in any outside suit vulnerable or non-vulnerable. However, if vulnerable some require a stopper in the other minor but no stoppers in the majors. Why? With no stoppers outside, partner will bid 4♣, asking partner to bid his minor. With all suits stopped, he will leave the bid stand. However, when vulnerable, partner only needs stoppers in the majors, knowing partner has a long minor and the other minor stopped he will leave the game bid of 3NT* to play if vulnerable with stoppers in the majors.

When responding to the Gambling 3NT* bid, Marty Bergen makes the following recommendations for responder bids.

Responses to 3NT* (Per Marty Bergen)

4♣ says let's play in a part score 4♣ or 4♦

4♦* is asking opener to bid a singleton: responses are:

4♥	heart singleton
4♠	spade singleton
4NT	minor suit singleton
5♣	no singleton

Example: Responder has   ♠ AKQ7 ♥ 76 ♦ AKQ7 ♣ 432

With a heart singleton, you want to play in six clubs otherwise you would bid five clubs.

4♥ and **4♠** are signoffs in responder's long suit. Opener must pass.

4NT is invitational to slam, asking opener to bid a minor suit slam with an outside trick.

5♣ asks opener to play in a minor suit game.

5♦ is a signoff by responder, responder knows that the opener has long diamonds and wants to play game from his side.

5NT is a grand slam try, to play in 7♣ or 7♦.

Responder has no losers outside the trump suit but is usually void of the trump suit and is afraid of a trump loser.

6♣ is to play slam in 6♣/6♦; opener is to pick the suit.
A bid of 6♦ by responder is to play slam in diamonds; responder knows that it is the long suit.

ACOL* 4NT Opening

An opening bid of 4NT asks for specific aces. The responses are:

5♣	no ace
5♦/5♥/5♠/6♣	shows the ace in the suit bid
5NT	shows 2 aces

(*) A bidding system played primarily in Great Britain.

Namyats

NAMYATS was created by Sam Stayman who, creator of the Stayman 2♣ convention, coined the NAMYATS Convention using his name in reverse order. The convention, part of the 2/1 Game Force System, allows one to differentiate between a strong distributional hand, which may provide a slam opportunity with less opponent interference, and a preemptive bid, which has no slam opportunity.

The bid requires a 7+ card suit in hearts or spades and like the strong two club opener in standard systems like 2/1 requires 8 ½ - 9 playing tricks. The major suit has two of the top three honors non-vulnerable and three of the top five honors vulnerable, and both require an outside ace or protected king. Thus, you almost have game in hand; partner has to only cover one loser in a major game contract. The bids use the minor preemptive four-level bids:

> 4♣*   transfer to hearts
> 4♦*   transfer to spades

If responder (partner) bids the transfer suit, this usually denotes no interest in slam. However, if one bids the next step, it indicates slam interest in the major.

> 4♣*   4♦ slam interest
> 4♦*   4♥ slam interest

*The bids are respectively 1430 Roman Keycard Blackwood bids using kickback. Opener does not bid the transfer suit but responds to the keycard ask. An example follows.

Opener   ♠AKQ109653 ♥7 ♦ 9 ♣ KJ7
Responder   ♠72 ♥ AK ♦ KQJ976 ♣ A102

The above hand is too strong to open 4♠. Playing Namyats, one would open the bidding 4♦*. With slam interest, responder bids 4♥ and with two keycards and the queen of trump, opener responds 5♦. Lacking one keycard, responders bids 6♠.

The Namyats bid is more descriptive than opening the hand 1♣.

Flannery Option

While we recommend one use the two-level bids of a major as weak, similar to the 2/1 Game Force System with OGUST responses; another option is to use the two-level bids to show values. With the "values" option, the bids are defined:

> 2♥   11-15 HCP and 5-4 in hearts and spades (Flannery)
> 2♠   11-15 HCP and 5-5 in spades and hearts

After the bid of two hearts, 2NT is the Flannery asking bid as in 2/1 Game Force and usually forcing to game. After the bid of two spades, the bid of 2NT is again forcing to game in a major or notrump, a simple raise would deny game values.

Chapter 9 – Opening 2♦* and 2♣*

Opening 2♦* (Mini-Roman Modified)

THE OPENING BID OF two diamonds is virtually never the same across strong club systems. In many systems it is used to show a very strong 4-4-4-1 with 16+ HCP. However, we have found that this bid does not occur that often, perhaps 1 percent of the time. Hence, we will use the bid to show a hand that is 4-4 in the majors and with a distribution that is exactly: 4=4-4-1 or 4=4-5-0. The bid must be alerted and described as being 4=4 in the majors with a singleton or void. This concept was suggested by Bill Amason.

Partner Response to 2♦*

2♥/2♠   3+ card support 0-12 HCP

2NT*   13+ HCP (asks partner to bid singleton)

             Opener
             Rebids
             3♣*/3♦* 4=4=4=1/4=4=1=4 singleton in bid suit
             4♣*/4♦* 4=4=5=0/4=4=0=5 void in bid suit
             Partner sets the contract or bids 4NT (Blackwood)

3♣/3♦   13+ HCP with own 5-card suit

             Opener
             Rebids
             Pass   11 HCP
             3NT   12+ HCP denies support for the minor
             Bidding other minor at the 4-level is an asking bid
             - bid best major

3♥/3♠	shows 13+ HCP and 4+ cards in major
3NT	16+ HCP and support for 1 major
4♣*/4♦*	splinter bid with singleton and support for 1 major
5♣*/5♦*	void in bid suit with support for 1 major

With interference

	Negative double through 3♠
	Redouble 10+ HCP
	Cuebid 13+ HCP

Opening 2♣*

The opening bid of two clubs in Precision shows 11-15 HCP and a 6+ clubs with or without a four-card major. This bid also must be alerted. Do not use the bid with only a five-card club suit. The responses to the bid follow.

Partner responses:

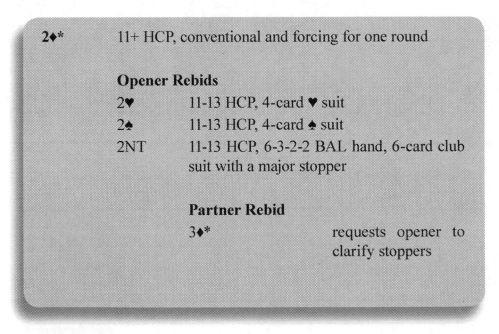

| 2♦* | 11+ HCP, conventional and forcing for one round |

Opener Rebids

2♥	11-13 HCP, 4-card ♥ suit
2♠	11-13 HCP, 4-card ♠ suit
2NT	11-13 HCP, 6-3-2-2 BAL hand, 6-card club suit with a major stopper

Partner Rebid

| 3♦* | requests opener to clarify stoppers |

Opener Bids

3♥*		♥ stopper
3♠*		♠ stopper
3NT		♥ and ♠ stoppers

3♣	14-15 HCP non-forcing and unbalanced hand (1-3-3-6)	
3♥	14-15 HCP, 5+card ♥ suit	
3♠	14-15 HCP, relay back to ♣s, solid club suit AKJ109x allows responder to bid 3NT	
3NT	14-15 HCP, 5+spades and 6+ clubs	

2♥/2♠	Natural with 5+cards, 8-10 HCP
2NT	Natural 10-12 HCP
3♣	Preemptive raise not forward going
3♦/3♥/3♠	6+ card suit, 12 HCP opener may pass, raise, or bid 3NT
4♣	Invitational to game in clubs
4♥/4♠	Natural and to play
4♦	RKCB for clubs

With interference

Negative double through 3♠

Redouble	10+ HCP
Cuebid	13+ HCP

BIDDING QUESTIONS

What is your opening bid?

(1) ♠ K986 ♥ QJ87 ♦ Q98 ♣ K5

(2) ♠ K976 ♥ QJ97 ♦ Q987 ♣ A

(3) ♠ A762 ♥ KQJ9 ♦ void ♣ KQ10542

(4) ♠ A6 ♥7 ♦ AK98 ♣ Q109542

(5) ♠ K93 ♥A7 ♦ K98 ♣ AJ952

(6) ♠ A762 ♥ KQJ ♦ void ♣ AKQ10542

(7) ♠ 76 ♥ Q8 ♦ 7 ♣ AKQJ10542

(1) You have 4=4-3-2 distribution and 11 HCP, open 1♦*.

(2) You have 4=4=4=1 distribution and 12 HCP, open 2♦*.

(3) You have 15 HCP with 6 clubs, open 2♣*.

(4) You have 13 HCP with 6 clubs, open 2♣*.

(5) You have a semi-balanced hand with 15 HCP, open 1NT.

(6) You have 19 HCP, open 1♣*.

(7) You have a long minor, open 3NT* (gambling).

Partner has opened 2♣* and 2♦*, so how do you respond?

(1) ♠ K986 ♥ QJ87 ♦ Q98 ♣ K5

With 11 HCP, and two four-card majors, after the bid of 2♣*, bid 2♦*. If partner shows either major or rebids clubs, you will pass. If opener responds 2NT, you should pass.

After the opening bid of 2♦*, you must bid 2♥.

(2) ♠ KQ6 ♥ AJ976 ♦ 98 ♣ K5

You have 13 HCP, after the bid of 2♣*, bid 3♥ (natural to play). If partner bids 3NT, pass.

After the bid of 2♦*, bid 2NT; after opener shows his singleton, bid 3♥ (invitational to game). With 15 HCP, you would have bid 4♥.

(3) ♠ K76 ♥ 976 ♦ A982 ♣ 876

You have only 7 HCP; after 2♣*, bid 3♣. This forces the opponents to the three-level.

After the bid of 2♦*, you should bid 2♠.

(4) ♠ K76 ♥ KJ97 ♦ A982 ♣ J7

You have 12 HCP; after 2♣*, bid 2NT. If partner bids spades, pass. However, if partner bids 3♥, bid four. After the bid of 3♦, you would invite game by bidding 3♥.

After the opening bid of 2♦*, you must bid 3♥.

(5) ♠ KQ76 ♥ J7 ♦ 75 ♣ AKQ86

You have 15 HCP; after the bid of 2♣*, bid 2♦* to see if you have a double fit in spades and clubs; if partner bids 3♠, bid 4♠ and if partner bids 3♥, bid 5♣.

After the bid of 2♦*, you should bid game in spades, 4♠.

COMPLETE EXAMPLES

(1) **Opener**   ♠ KQ76 ♥ J7 ♦ 7 ♣ AKQ862   **Partner**   ♠ A102 ♥ KQ9865 ♦ 953 ♣ J

Opener has 14 HCP and a six-card club suit and opens 2♣*. Partner has 10 HCP and a five-card heart suit and bids 2♦*; opener next bids 2♠* to show his four-card spade suit. With his six-card heart suit, partner next bids 3♥; opener bids 4♥.

(2) **Opener**   ♠ 76 ♥ AQ7 ♦ 105 ♣ AKJ1052   **Partner**   ♠ KJ54 ♥ 98 ♦ AK94 ♣ Q73

With a six-card club suit and 14 HCP, opener bids 2♣*. With four spades, partner bids 2♦* (asking for a four-card major). Without a major, opener next bids 2NT (showing 6-3-2-2 distribution). Partner bids 3♦*, and opener next bids 3♥* (heart stopper); partner next bids 3NT. Note, if partner did not have a heart stopper, the final contract would be 5♣.

(3) **Opener**   ♠ AQ76 ♥ KQJ2 ♦ J1095 ♣ 7   **Partner**   ♠ K532 ♥ 98 ♦ K943 ♣ KJ6

With 4=4-4-1 distribution and 13 HCP, open the bidding 2♦*. Partner has 10 HCP and bids 2♠. If partner had the following hand with 11 HCP ♠ K5 ♥ 98 ♦ K10432 ♣ KQ72, what is his bid? You cannot bid a major, bid 2NT.

(4) **Opener**   ♠ AQ76 ♥ AK95 ♦ 7 ♣ 10954   **Partner**   ♠ KJ52 ♥ Q8 ♦ AK4 ♣ KJ76

With 4=4-1-4, distribution, open 2♦*. Partner has 17 HCP and support for one of the majors. He bids 3NT. Because of his singleton diamond, opener next bids 4♠.

Chapter 10 – Opening 1♦*

THE BID OF 1♦* in the Precision System is a catchall bid and must be alerted. You do not have a five-card major, your hand is not balanced or too weak for 1NT, and you do not have a long club suit, but you usually have at least 2+ diamonds (sometimes only one, for example 4-3-1=5) and 11-15 HCP (11-13 HCP non-vulnerable and 12-15 vulnerable and two quick tricks). This is used when no other Precision bid is available. In the fourth seat, the rule of 15 is used.

The bid of 1♦* will always show one of the following hand-types with two quick tricks:

- Balanced or semi-balanced hands in the 11-12 point range (like a weak notrump!)
- 11-15 points with a weak five-card clubs suit and likely a four-card diamond suit
- 11-15 point hands with any five-card or longer diamond suit not covered by other opening standard Precision openings
- Some 4-4-4-1 hands that are 4=4 in the majors but 16+ HCP

In many books on Precision, hands that are 4=4 in the majors with 11-15 HCP are opened 1♦*. This is not the case in Precision Simplified; those hands are instead opened 2♦*. A hand that is not 4=4 in the majors, for example:

♠ 654 ♥ AQJ7 ♦ 65 ♣ AJ97

would be opened 1♦*. You have 2+ diamonds and 12 HCP and no five-card major. Another hand that is opened 1♦* is one that is 4-5 in the minors with five clubs and four diamonds. Or, adding a club and deleting a diamond:

♠ 654 ♥ AQJ7 ♦ 6 ♣ AJ975,

you again must open the hand 1♦*, even with only a singleton diamond.

If you had the hand:

♠ 7 ♥ QJ7 ♦ AKJ7 ♣ Q5432

you would again open the bidding 1♦*. After partner bids 1♠ or 1NT, show your club suit by bidding 2♣. Partner knows it does not contain six-cards since you did not open the hand 2♣*.

Because the opponents like to interfere over the bid of one diamond almost as much as the bid of 1♣*, we recommend the use of relay bids for the majors and notrump. The bidding structure follows.

When they double

If the bidding goes: 1♦* - **double** bid as follows:

REDOUBLE   shows 5+ hearts   asks partner to bid 1♥

1♥   shows 5+ spades   asks partner to bid 1♠

1♠   transfer bid   asks partner to bid 1NT

1NT   8-10 HCP

2♣   natural 5+ clubs

2♦   13+ HCP, diamond raise

2♥/2♠   to Play

2NT   11-12 HCP

3♣   10-12 HCP, limit raise in diamonds

Responding to 1♦*

The Precision responses to the bid of one diamond are similar to the bids used playing 2/1. The bidding structure follows and includes inverted minors with crisscross. However, with a **16+ HCP we use strong jump shifts** bid for a major which differs from 2/1 where jump shifts are usually weak.

The bids follow.

1♥/1♠ 4+ cards in suit with 6+ HCP (to show weak hand rebid majors since using strong jump shifts)

1NT   8-10 HCP, balanced hand

2NT   11- 12 HCP, balanced hand

3NT   13-15 HCP, balanced hand

2♣   13+ HCP forcing one round

2♦*   13+ HCP with 6+ diamonds forcing one round

2♥/2♠   16+ HCP strong jump shift in Major 5+ cards. (GF)

3♣*   10-12 HCP, 6+ diamonds (Crisscross)

3♦*   less than 10 HCP, weak, preemptive raise 5+ ♦

3♥/3♠	Splinter bid in support of diamonds (slam interest 16+)
4♣	Splinter bid in support of diamonds (slam interest 16+)
4♦	Minorwood 1430 Keycard for diamonds
4♥/4♠	Single-suited hand to play

After a strong jump shift in a major, one either plays the hand in the major, notrump or perhaps diamonds.

After 1♦* -1♥

Opener re-bids

1♠	4 spades, denies 4 hearts
1NT	balanced hand, denies a 4-card major
2♣	shows 5 clubs, denies a 4-card major
2♦	5+ diamonds, denies a 4-card major
2♥	11- 12 HCP, 3+ card support
2NT	13-15 HCP, stoppers in other suits
3♣	5-5 in the minors (values in the minors)
3♦	6+ diamond suit (strong diamond suit)
3♥	13- 15 HCP and 4 hearts

The bids after the sequence 1♦*-1♠ follow similarly.

New Minor Forcing (Checkback Stayman)

The sequence 1♦* - 1♥/1♠ - 1NT - 2♣ is New Minor Forcing or Checkback Stayman.

In particular, suppose the bidding goes: 1♦* - 1♥ - 1NT - 2♣ - (?)

2♦	no heart fit 11-12 HCP
2♥	3 hearts and 11-12 HCP
2♠	4 spades and 13-15 HCP
2NT	13-15 HCP and balanced
3♥	3 hearts and 13-15 HCP

The bids after the sequence 1♦* - 1♠ - 1NT - 2♣ - (?) follow similarly.

To invoke New Minor Forcing requires 10+ HCP, hence, if it not used, the opening bidder knows immediately that partner has less than 10 HCP and thus any rebid by partner is usually passed. However, a jump rebids (at the three-level) by the responder in a major are invitational to game showing 11-12 HCP as is the bid of 2NT.

After the bid of a major, a jump to the three-level in a minor shows a major-minor two-suited hand usually 5-5 with no more than six losers.

Getting to notrump

After an inverted minor raise 1♦* - pass - 2♦* (showing 13+ HCP).
1. Show major suit stoppers 2♥ or 2♠, bid up-the-line. No extra values.
2. Bid **2NT** with a minimum and both majors are stopped.
3. Bid **3♣** to show club stopper, neither hearts of spades stopped.
4. Bid **3♦** with a minimum without major stoppers.
5. Bid **3♥** or **3NT**, showing hearts stopped, over **2♠** with minimum values.

After a weak raise 1♦* - pass - 3♦* (showing less than 10 HCP)

a. Pass with all minimum and almost all intermediate sized hands
b. A new suit is forcing one round and shows a very strong hand
c. **3NT** is to play regardless what partner had for his preemptive raise
d. **4 of the minor** is invitational

Note: After **1♦*-2♦*,** you can bid major stoppers **out of order** to show club shortness below **3NT**. Opener bids **2♠** and then, over a **2NT** or **3♦** response, bids **3♥**. This shows club shortness and enough values for game while still allowing **3NT** to be bid by partner.

ILLUSTRATIONS, BIDDING QUESTIONS, AND EXAMPLES

Let's look at some hands where you must open 1♦*.

(1) ♠ 65 ♥ A7 ♦ AKQ9 ♣ J9876

You have five clubs and four diamonds and 12 HCP. You cannot open it 2♣ with only five. If partner bids one of a major, rebid 2♣ to show five. Even though you are 5-4 in the minors, you cannot show this without rebids.

(2) ♠ Q98 ♥ K654 ♦ Q4 ♣ AJ987

You have 12 HCP and again would open it one diamond. If partner bids hearts, you would support the bid; however, if partner bids 1♠, you would again bid 2♣. Note that here you have shortness in diamonds. If partner next bids diamonds, bid notrump.

(3) ♠98 ♥ J ♦ AKJ43 ♣ AJ987

You have 14 HCP and are 5-5 in the minors. If partner responds one of a major, you would next jump in clubs and bid 3♣ which shows you are 5-5 in the minors with values in the minors.

(4) ♠98 ♥ J ♦ AKQJ432 ♣ A109

You have 15 HCP and a very strong diamond suit; after partner bids a major, respond with a jump bid of 3♦ to show a strong 6+ diamond suit. If partner has the other major, it encourages 3NT. Do not open the hand 3NT with the A♣ in first seat.

(5) ♠987 ♥ J987 ♦ A ♣ AQJ109

This is a difficult hand for the Precision System. It does not fit any bidding structure. You have three options: (1) pass with 12 HCP and wait to see what develops, (2) by agreement open the bidding 1♥ with only four, or (3) open the hand 1♦.

(6) ♠K987 ♥ A987 ♦ A3 ♣ KQJ

Even with 17 HCP, open the bidding 1♦*. If you open the bidding 1♣* and partner bids 1♦*, what is your rebid? Perhaps 1NT!

If partner raises the bid of one diamond, plan to play the hand in notrump

(7) ♠AJ7 ♥ 7 ♦ AJ10 765 ♣ 567

You have two aces and only 10 HCP, open the bidding 1♦* and then rebid them to show your length. This is a minimum Precision opening, you have a six-card suit with a singleton, do not pass.

(8) ♠7 ♥ KQ98 ♦ AKJ6 ♣ K567

You have 16 HCP open the hand 1♦*. If you were to open it 1♣* and partner were to bid 1♦*, you have no rebid because of the singleton spade. If partner responds 1♥ after the bid of one diamond, you may bid 3♥.

(9) ♠K1085 ♥ KQ9 ♦ 7 ♣ A9754

You have 12 HCP, but only five clubs and you are not 4-4 in the majors. Even with a singleton diamond, you must open the hand one diamond. If your partner raises diamonds or bids notrump, play the hand in notrump. If partner preempts with the bid of 3♦, pass.

Your partner has opened the bidding 1♦*, what is your bid?

(1) ♠98 ♥ J ♦ AKJ43 ♣ AJ987

You have 14 HCP and five diamonds; to show your values, bid 2♦* (inverted) to show 13+ and diamonds. If partner bids 2♥ (stopper), bid 3♣ (stopper) trying to get to notrump.

(2) ♠98 ♥ J ♦ AQJ43 ♣ A10987

You only have 12 HCP and diamonds, bid 3♣* to show a limit raise in diamonds; if partner next bids 2NT (stoppers in both major), bid 3NT.

(3) ♠7 ♥ AQJ4 ♦ AKJ43 ♣ A7

You have 19 HCP, bid 3♠ (a splinter bid in support of diamonds showing 16+ HCP) and invitational to slam in diamonds.

(4) ♠7 ♥ AQJ42 ♦ AKJ4 ♣ A7

You again have 19 HCP, but with five hearts. Make a jump shift bid of 2♥ to show your values. If partner supports hearts, begin a cuebidding sequence or because of your singleton, use EKCB by bidding spades at the five-level. Do not use RKCB with a singleton.

(5) ♠AK64 ♥ 7 ♦ AKJ4 ♣ AK987

You have 22 HCP, bid 2♦*. Even with only four diamonds show 13+ HCP. Wait to see what partner next bids (some may splinter in hearts). You clearly have slam.

Bid each of the following hands.

| (1) | Opener | ♠ KQ76 ♥ J7 ♦ 78 ♣ AKQ86 |
| | Partner | ♠ A102 ♥ KQ9865 ♦ 953 ♣ J |

You have 15 HCP and two doubletons, open the bidding 1♦*. Partner will bid 1♥. Your rebid is 2♣. If partner rebids 2♥, then your bid is 2♠. Partner with four spades will bid 2♠ and you will bid game in spades.

| (2) | Opener | ♠ 73 ♥ J7 ♦ AQ54 ♣ AK986 |
| | Partner | ♠ A102 ♥ KQ98 ♦ K632 ♣ J2 |

You have 14 HCP, open the bidding open 1♦*. Partner with 13 HCP bids 1♥. Next opener will bid 2♣; followed by a bid of 2♠ (fourth suit forcing for one round). You would next bid 3NT.

Chapter 11 – Opening 2NT*

IN MANY VERSIONS OF Precision, the opening bid of 2NT shows 22-23 HCP and a balanced hand. In our version, with a negative response, this is accomplished by bidding 1♣* - 1♦* - 2NT*; with a positive response and no fit in the major, 1♣* - 2♦*/1♥*, or using the notrump transfer (1♣*-1♠*), one bids 3NT to show 22-23 HCP and a balanced hand.

In Precision Simplified, 2NT* is used to show a hand that is 5-5 in the minors with limited values. To open a hand 2NT* non-vulnerable requires only 5-10 HCP and vulnerable requires 11-15 HCP. These do not follow the bids in "Precision Today," the responses to the bid are:

Responses to 2NT* 5-5 in the minors

3♣ or 3♦ is to play
3♥* is an asking bid.

Opener Rebids (all bids are alerted)	
3♠	5-5 minimum (5-10 NV; 11-15 VUL)
3NT	maximum
4♣	6-5 (clubs, diamonds), minimum
4♦	6-5 (diamonds, clubs), minimum
4♥	6-5 (clubs, diamonds), maximum
4♠	6-5 (diamonds, clubs), maximum
4NT	6-6 in the minors

3♠   to play
3NT   to play
4♣/4♦ preemptive bids, to play
4♥/4♠ to play
5♣/5♦ to play

The bid of 2NT* is designed to be preemptive, game is unlikely. The strategy is to make bidding by the opponents difficult. The better your shape, the higher you should bid.

EXAMPLES

For each of the following hands, partner opens 2NT*, what is your bid, both (a) vulnerable (11-15) and (b) non-vulnerable (5-10)?

(1) ♠AK64 ♥ 7 ♦ AKJ4 ♣ AK987

You have 20 HCP. (a) With a great minor suit fit, bid 6♣. (b) Invite game by bidding 4♣.

(2) ♠ A102 ♥ AQ98 ♦ 9532 ♣ K2

You have 13 HCP, (a) bid 3♥, if partner is at a maximum with 15 HCP, he will bid 3NT and you would pass. With a minimum (11HCP), he will bid 3♠, and your rebid is 4♦. (b) Your only bid is 3♦ to play.

(3) ♠ KJ2 ♥ AQJ9865 ♦ A9 ♣ K

You have 18 HCP, (a) you know partner has at least 11 HCP, bid 4♥. (b) Because 3♥ is an asking bid, you cannot bid 3♥; bid 3NT to play.

(4) ♠ AQ9 ♥ A976 ♦ AQ9 ♣ A65

You have a balanced hand with 20 HCP, (a) or (b) bid 3NT.

(5) ♠ AQ98 ♥ AKQJ ♦ A9 ♣ K62

You are 4-4 in the majors with 23 HCP, (a) bid 3♥; if partner next bids 3♠, bid 3NT. However, if partner bids 3NT, bid 6NT. (b) Bid 3NT to play.

Chapter 12 – Slam Bidding

To reach a slam, the partnership should have about 33 HCP. In addition to a trump fit and count, slams require controls (aces, kings, voids, and singletons). The more controls between the partners, the easier the slam. To evaluate whether or not the partnership has the required controls, one uses cuebids and Blackwood Conventions. Blackwood Conventions reveal how many aces and kings, for example, while cuebidding or control showing bids reveal where they reside. Parts of this chapter appeared in Timm (2010), "2/1 Game Force a Modern Approach," however, the examples have been modified to fit into the Precision bidding structure.

The Blackwood Convention

The most used and abused convention in bridge is the original Blackwood Convention developed by Easley Blackwood Sr. because many believe it will handle all situations. It does not. While the convention does not require knowing the trump suit, it does require that one knows whether or not slam is possible. The convention augments this knowledge by helping one find the number of aces and kings.

The convention should not be used when:

(1) Holding two or more cards in an unbid suit with no ace or king (e.g., xx, Qx, Jx)

(2) Holding a void

(3) One has a slam invitational hand (e.g., 1NT facing 1NT hands)

To use the convention, the captain bids 4NT, which is the asking partner for the number of aces held.

The responses are:

5♣	0 aces or all 4 aces
5♦	1 ace
5♥	2 aces
5♠	3 aces

If only two aces are missing, the captain signs off in 5NT or five of a suit. If one ace is missing, one may bid 6NT or six of a suit.

What do you do if you have a void? Do not count it as an ace. With an even number of aces (2 or 4) bid 5NT and with an odd number (1 or 3), bid the suit at the six-levels. It works. **If you have no aces and a void (ignore the void),** bid 5♣ since the void may be in a suit where partner has an ace.

Knowing you have all the aces, 5NT is the king's ask (without a void response); the responses are:

6♣	0 kings or all 4 kings
6♦	1 king
6♥	2 kings
6♠	3 kings

Having all the aces and kings, one is in the grand slam zone; recall it requires roughly 37 Bergen points.

The major problem with the Blackwood Convention is you have no way of knowing about the ace and king of trump and the specific location of aces is unknown. To solve these shortcomings, one uses cuebids and the Roman Keycard Blackwood Convention, which has replaced the Blackwood Convention.

Roman Keycard Blackwood (RKCB) Convention - 1430

The most authoritative book (in my opinion) on this convention is by Eddie Kantar (2008), "Roman Keycard Blackwood the Final Word" 5th Edition, Master Point Press, Toronto, Ontario, Canada.

To use the RKCB convention, one must have agreed upon a trump suit. Knowing the trump suit, there are two Roman Keycard Conventions known as 1430 and 3014. When the strong hand asks, Mr. Kantar recommends that one play the 1430 version (marked as 1430 on the convention card); if the weak hand asks, he recommends 3014 (marked as RCK on the convention card). While Mr. Kantar has several criteria to determine which hand is considered strong and which hand is the weak hand, because more often than not the strong hand usually asks, we recommend always using the 1430 Roman Keycard Convention. Let's not get too complicated, unless you have an established partnership.

When using the RKCB convention, there are now five keycards, the four aces, and the king of trump. Another keycard is the queen of trump. If you do not use kickback (to be explained later), the 1430 RKCB ask is again 4NT. The responses are:

> 5♣   1 or 4 keycards (the 14 step)
>
> 5♦   3 or 0 keycards (the 30 step)
>
> 5♥   2 (or 5) keycards without the queen of trump in the agreed upon suit
>
> 5♠   2 (or 5) keycards with the queen of trump in the agreed upon suit

When one responds five clubs or five diamonds, the queen ask may be needed. After the response five clubs, the bid of 5♦ is the queen ask (when hearts or spades are the agreed upon trump suit). After the bid of five diamonds, the bid of 5♥ is the queen asks.

Queen Asks

In review, after five clubs and five diamonds, the queen asks are:

5♦ and 5♥   Queen asks

Responding to the 5♦ ask

(1) If you **do not** hold the queen, responder **returns to the agreed upon suit at the five-level.**

(2) **5NT shows the queen but no outside king!**

(3) With both (queen of trump and one or two kings), bid at the six-level of the lowest ranking king

Responding to the 5♥ ask

If you do not hold the queen, pass; with the queen, bid 5NT. With the queen and a king in the lower ranking suit, bid the suit. If it is a higher ranking king, return to the six-level.

King Asks

Knowing you hold all the aces, and king-queen of trump (note some players do not require holding the queen), **5NT is the specific kings ask!**

The specific king ask is needed for a grand slam try in the agreed upon suit or notrump.
Responses are:

(1) Return to the agreed upon trump suit at the six-level denies any kings.

(2) With two kings, bid the cheapest at the six-level (below agreed upon trump suit); if the king is of higher rank, return to the trump suit at the six-level.

(3) With three kings, bid 6NT.

To find a second king below the trump suit, bid the suit. Without the second king, responder bids the trump suit at the six-level.

With the king, bid as follows:

(1) Make a first step response, including 6NT with Kxx(x).

(2) Make a second step response with Kxx.

(3) Raise the ask suit with Kx.

Playing 1430 RKCB, the standard is to use the specific king ask; however, some still may play the number of kings from "Blackwood" excluding the trump suit –YOU BETTER ASK your partner.

Responding with voids

Using the 1430 convention and having a void, the responses to 4NT are:

5NT = 2 or 4 an even number of keycards with a void **(with zero ignore the void)**
6 of suit below the trump suit = odd number keycards (1/3)

6 trump suit = odd number of keycards (1/3) with a void in higher ranking suit

Specific Suit Asks (SSA)

We have seen that one may ask for keycards, the queen of trump, and having both, ask for specific kings. When searching for a grand slam, one may also need to know about an outside suit (not the trump suit). For example, do you have a queen in the suit, a doubleton, or a singleton? To ask and answer this question, one makes a Specific Suit Ask (SSA).

The specific suit asks is generally done when the captain has the queen of trump after the keycard responses of 5♣ or 5♦.

> After 5♣   6♣, 6♦ is SSA
>
> After 5♦   5♠, 6♦, 6♥ is SSA

The responses are:

Make a first step response, including 6NT with third-round control Qx(x), Ax, AQx, xx

Make a second step response with second-round control Kxx(x)

Make a third step response with Kx

Raise the ask bid with KQx and JUMP to the trump suit with a singleton

Over Interference DOPI-ROPI or DEPO

When the opponents interfere, most players play DOPI/ROPI. Another option is to use DEPO. While most do not use both, I recommend the use of both, which depends on the level of interference.

If the opponents interfere at the five-levels with a bid, use DOPI,

Double	1 keycard
Pass	0 keycards
1st Step suit above	2 keycards
2nd Step up	3 keycards

If the opponents interfere at the five-levels with a double, use ROPI,

Re-Double	1 keycard
Pass	0 keycards
1st Step suit above	2 keycards
2nd Step up	3 keycards

If the opponents interfere at the **six levels**, use DEPO,

Double	even number of keycards (0, 2, 4)
Pass	odd number of keycards (1, 3)

Kickback or Redwood and Minorwood

When the agreed upon suit is a minor, the use of 4NT as a keycard ask will often get the responses too high. To avoid this problem, one uses Roman Keycard Blackwood with kickback. It works as follows: if clubs is trump, then 4♦ is used to ask. If diamonds is trump, the 4♥ is used to ask. If hearts is trump, either 4♠ (in order to avoid problems with the queen ask) or 4NT is used to ask. When spades is trump, one always uses 4NT to ask.

One responds to the ask using each suit in order. For example, suppose the agreed upon suit is diamonds so 4♥ is the ask, the responses are:

4♠	1 or 4 keycards (the 14 step)	**step 1**
4NT	3 or 0 keycards (the 30 step)	**step 2**
5♣	2 (or 5) keycards w/o queen of trump in agreed suit	**step 3**
5♦	2 (or5) keycards w/o queen of trump in agreed suit	**step 4**

What is the queen ask? After 4♠ it is 4NT and after 4NT, it is 5♣! Note that with no queen, you again return to the five-level of the agreed upon trump suit. If you have the queen, bid six. It works! All extensions follow.

Instead of playing Kickback or Redwood, some partnerships play **Minorwood.** The Minorwood Convention uses four of the agreed minor for the RKCB ask. For example, in the auction 1♦ - 2♦, the bid of 4♦ is Minorwood; it is used instead of 4♥, Kickback, or Redwood. It can also be played in a sequence when Kickback may be confusing. For example, if the bid of 4♠ is confusing, one may jump into four of a minor instead of using Kickback RKCB. I have seen this called the "Bothwood" convention.

Slam Bidding with No Agreed Upon Suit

When playing 1430 RKC, how should one proceed if there is no prior agreement on the trump suit? Some recommend that (1) it should always be the last-bid suit, some suggest that (2) one should not play any form of RKC, but instead simply use Blackwood as an ace only ask (no keycards), others recommend (3) that RKC be used only if the last-bid suit is a minor (opener or responder) but not a major, and some play (4) that it is the last-bid suit of the responder. What is your agreement?

The approach you use must be discussed with your partner when you make out your convention card. There is no "best" or standard approach. Let's look at an example.

Opener	Responder
♠KQJ863	♠A2
♥K10942	♥J7
♦Q8	♦AK5
♣Void	♣AKQJ104

The bidding goes:

Opener	Responder
1♠	2♣
2♥	3♦
3♥	4NT
6♣	7NT
Pass	

Responder leaps to 4NT to ask for keycards. Since the last-bid suit was hearts, opener bids 6♣ which shows an odd number of keycards, the king of hearts, and a void in clubs.

Thinking that the one keycard is the A♥, responder bids a grand slam, 7NT. Whose fault? The fault was that they lacked an agreement as to what 4NT means when there is no agreed upon suit.

Note, if you play the last-bid suit you will only survive a 4NT ask when you intend to play in your own suit as long as you hold the king of the last-bid suit. Partner is forced to answer only aces! In the previous example, responder did not hold the king. Because there was no agreed upon suit, one would bid 5♣ (zero keycards). Partner would bid 6NT.

The above example suggests that one use Blackwood if there is no agreed upon suit.

To illustrate, suppose the bidding goes one heart-two clubs - two hearts - 4NT. Then, since the last-bid minor suit of responder was clubs, 4NT agrees clubs. If responder wanted to agree hearts, and the partnership plays that a raise to three hearts is forcing; it is easy enough to bid three hearts and then 4NT. If a raise to three hearts is not forcing, then a jump to four diamonds agrees hearts, and if partner bids four hearts, 4NT can be bid. If the responder wants to agree spades, he bids two spades or three spades, and then bids 4NT.

Thus, if you do not have an agreed upon suit, you can play Blackwood or agree that one may play the last-bid minor suit of opener or responder.

With no agreed upon suit, here are my suggestions.

1. Use keycard after any four-level bid.

2. All Kickback auctions are RKCB.

3. If two suits are agreed upon, the **FIRST SUIT BID** is trumps for RKCB purposes.

4. When none of the above applies, use Blackwood as ace only asks.

Overview: Roman Keycard Blackwood 1430(&)

4NT when hearts or spades is the agreed upon suit (Keycard Ask)

5♣	1 or 4 keycards
5♦	0 or 3 keycards
5♥	2 or 5 keycards without the queen of trump
5♠	2 or 5 keycards with the queen of trump or holding a fifth trump

Kickback

Use 4♦ as keycard ask when CLUBS is the agreed upon suit

Use 4♥ as keycard ask when DIAMONDS is the agreed upon suit

Voids

5NT = 2 or 4 an even number of keycards with a void (with 0 ignore the void)

6 of suit below the trump suit = odd number keycards (1/3)

6 trump suit = odd number of keycards (1/3) with a void in higher ranking suit

DOPI/ROPI   Interference at the five-level

DBL/RE-DBL: 0 or 3 keycards

PASS: 1 or 4 keycards

DEPO Interference at the six-level

DBL: Even Number of keycards (0/2/4)

PASS: Odd Number of keycards (1/3)

QUEEN ASK: After 5♣, **5♦** is queen ask   **AND**   After 5♦, **5♥** is queen ask

Responses:

> **Denial:** Return to the 5-level of the agreed upon suit
>
> **6-Level of agreed Suit:** With queen and **no** side-suit king or extra trump
>
> **6-Level of Lower King Suit:** With queen and 1/2 side-suit kings
>
> **5NT:** With queen **without** a side-suit king, but trump extra

5NT is a Specific King ASK (NOT NUMBER OF KINGS)

YES: Bid Lowest King Suit BELOW the agreed upon trump suit.

NO: Return to the agreed upon trump suit (or king is above agreed trump suit).

To ask for a SECOND king, the asker bids the suit.

Without, return to the agreed suit.

Holding a SECOND king

> Make a first step response, including 6NT with Kxx(x)
> Make a second step response with Kxx
>
> Raise the ask suit with Kx

SPECIFIC SUIT ASK (SSA) After 5♣: 5♥, 6♣, 6♦ is SSA. After 5♦: 5♠, 6♦, 6♥ is SSA

Make a 1st step response, including 6NT with third-round control Qx(x), Ax, AQx, xx

Make a 2nd step response with second-round control Kxx(x)

Make a 3rd step response with Kx

Raise the ask bid with KQx and JUMP to the trump suit with a singleton

(&) With NO AGREED upon SUIT some use the standard BLACKWOOD CONVENTION for Ace Asking and 5NT for NUMBER of King's Ask

Let's consider some examples on the use of RKCB

Slam 1
Opener   ♠A7   ♥AQ65 ♦84 ♣AKQ98
Responder   ♠KQ5 ♥ K843 ♦KQJ6 ♣7

Opener	Responder
1♣*	2NT*
3♣	3♥
4♥	4NT
5♦	5♥
6♣	6♥

The opener has 17 HCP and partner bids 2NT showing 14+ HCP. After Stayman, a heart fit is found. Finding the heart fit, responder bids 4NT (alternatively, he could use Kickback and ask by bidding 4♠). The response of 5♦ shows 0 or 3 keycards. The bid of 5♥ is the queen asks. The bid of 6♣ shows the Q♥ and the K♣. Opener bids the slam 6♥.

In this example, we did not use Kickback, but we should have because it may be difficult to determine if the bid of 5♥ is sign-off or queen ask. Instead of bidding 4NT, suppose one bids 4♠; we would then have:

Opener	Partner
1♣*	2NT*
3♣	3♥
4♥	4♠
5♣	5♦
6♣	6♥

Now, 5♣ shows 0 or 3 keycards and 5♦ becomes the queen ask. Denying the queen, the bid would be 5♥, which is short of game. However, 6♣ shows the queen plus the king of clubs. Responder again bids 6♥.

Slam 2
Opener   ♠AJ7 ♥AQJ753 ♦AQ8 ♣7
Responder   ♠K5 ♥ K1084 ♦8765 ♣AK9

Opener	Partner
1♣*	2NT*
3♥	4♥
4NT	5♥
5NT	6♣
6♦	6♥

Opener has 18 HCP and partner has 13 HCP.

After the bid of 1♣*, responder bids 2NT* showing a balanced hand with 14+ HCP. Opener next shows his five-card heart suit, and partner supports the suit. Opener next bids 4NT. With two keycards, the bid is 5♥. Opener has the queen of trump, bids 5NT, which is the specific king ask. With the K♣, responder bids 6♣. The bid of 6♦ is the second king's ask. Without the king, responder again signs off in the heart slam.

Slam 3
Opener   ♠AJ7   ♥AQJ753 ♦AQ87 ♣ void
Responder ♠K5   ♥ K1084 ♦10965 ♣AK9

You have the same hand, but now you have a void. You cannot bid 4NT with a void. However, you have two options, cuebidding or using another convention called Exclusion Keycard Blackwood (EKCB). Because cuebidding a void can be dangerous, we consider EKCB.

Exclusion Roman Keycard Blackwood (EKCB) Convention

The convention is only played when a known major suit agreement is a major and you know you are in the region of slam. For example, after a Jacoby 2NT bid, a concealed splinter bid, or perhaps a Swiss bid. The convention may also be played whenever the last-bid suit is a major (with or without an agreement). The convention is initiated by an unusual jump to the five-level above game in your void suit. You are asking for keycards for the agreed upon major or the last-bid major excluding the void suit. Partner does not count the ace in the void suit bid; now, there are only four keycards, three aces, and a king. **There is no such thing as 1430 or 3014 EKCB.** The responses are steps above the bid suit.

Responses to EKCB

First Step	0 keycards
Second Step	1 keycard
Third Step	2 keycards without the queen
Fourth Step	2 keycards with the queen
Fifth Step	3 keycards (very unusual)

The only exception to a five-level bid is that one may use 4♠ if you agree that hearts is trump at the two-levels. However, you cannot do this if you play Kickback. Thus, I would only recommend that it be used with bids at the five-levels.

As with 1430 RKCB, the bid of 5NT is again the specific king ask. The next step after a 0 or 1, including the void suit (but excluding 5NT) is the queen ask. Finally, the bid of any suit that is not the queen ask is the SSA.

What do you do after an EKCB ask with a void? You must always ignore it.

Returning to our Slam 3 example, opener bids 5♣ (EKCB). Excluding the club suit, responder has one keycard (king of hearts) and bids 5♦. Partner, having all the aces and a void in clubs, knows it is the K♥. Having the queen, what next? He next bids 5NT, which is again the specific king ask; without the king of diamonds, partner again signs off in six hearts.

Let's now look at the Slam 3 example.

Opener	♠AJ7 ♥AQJ753 ♦AQ87 ♣ void
Responder	♠K5 ♥ K1084 ♦10965 ♣AK9

The bidding would go as follows using EKCB.

1♣	1♠#
1NT	2♣ (Stayman)
2♥	3♥
5♣ (EKCB)	5♦ (0 keycards, excluding clubs)
5♥	6♥ (2 club controls)

Alternatively, one may use cuebids.

1♣	1♠#
1NT	2♣ (Stayman)
2♥	3♥
4♦ (cuebid)	5♣ (cuebid)
5♠ (cuebid)	6♣ (second cuebid)
6♥	

Grand Slam Force (GSF) after 1NT – is the bid of 5NT. It may be used after a notrump opening or after one has agreed upon a suit.

To use the bid after a one notrump opening requires 22+ HCP. If opener is at the top of his bid (15 HCP), then bid 7NT; otherwise, they bid 6NT.

After a suit bid, for example, 1♠ - 5NT or 4♥ - 5NT, with two or more controls in the bid suit, partner bids:

- **6 of the agreed trump suit** if holding **1** of the top 3 trump honors (e.g., the ace)

- **7 of the agreed trump suit** if holding **2** of the top 3 trump honors (e.g., the king and queen)

A more complicated schedule of responses may be used that asks partner to describe his trump holding more precisely.

6♣	ace or king of trump
6♦	queen of trump
6♥	no honor, but extra trump length
6♠	no honor or extra trump length
7♣/7trump suit	2 of the top 3 honors

When the agreed upon suit is a minor, 5NT is again used as a Grand Slam Force (it requires that partner has two top honors); however, 5♠ is now the GSF bid when you only need one top honor (A/K/Q).

Pick a Slam - Without a known fit or when the opponents interfere, a jump to 5NT is used to ask partner to pick slam. For example, the bidding may go: 1♣* - 1♥; 2♦ - 5NT or the bidding may go 2♣* - 3♠; 4♣ - 5NT.

Declaratory-Interrogatory 4NT

Instead of using EKCB that uses the five-level bid, the Blue Italian Club team used a jump to 4NT after a suit agreement called the Declaratory-Interrogatory 4NT bid, also called DI 4NT. It is both a telling and asking bid. When used after a suit agreement, it says:
1. I have two first round controls (usually two aces but may include a void).
2. I have an ace/king in all skipped suits except the one of lowest rank, and extra values.

The bid asks:

1. Do you have at least one round control in the agreed upon suit?

2. Do you have additional values and slam interest?

Observe that DI 4NT is a multiple cuebid showing both aces and controls.

We again look at our Slam 3 example using DI 4NT.

1♣	1♠#
1NT	2♣ (Stayman)
2♥	3♥
4NT DI	5♣ (cuebid, positive response)
5♦ (cuebid)	6♣ (second cuebid)
6♥	

The responses to a DI bid may be negative or positive. The negative response is to simply return to the trump suit at the five-level. A positive response is to show a control (ace or king) in a lower ranking suit or a jump to slam with a higher ranking control.

Double Agreement Roman Keycard Blackwood (DRKCB)

With a double agreement, there are now six keycards (four aces and two kings), NOT FIVE, so we have what are called Double agreement 1430 Roman Keycard Blackwood (DRKCB). We consider DRKCB responses for some double agreements.
Major-Major Agreements

a)	Opener	Responder	b)	Opener	Responder
	1♠	2♥		1♥	2♠
	3♣	3♠		3♠	4♥
	4♥	4NT		4NT	

Then 4NT is a DRKCB ask.

When responding to DRKCB asks, there are now six keycards. And, **there are no void-showing responses.** The first two responses (5♣ and 5♦) of DRKCB are the same as 1430 RKCB; however, there are now three queens showing responses:

5♥	2 with neither queen
5♠	2 with one queen
5NT	2 with both queens

Note that in the second step (5♠), you do not know which queen. However, if partner makes a first or second step response to a DRKCB ask (5♣ and 5♦), unless the asker has both of the agreed upon suit queens, the queen situation is unknown. To now ask about queens, the asker uses the next available "free bid" step, excluding the trump suits, but including 4NT for a queen ask. The four-response steps now become:

1st step	2 with no queen
2nd step	2 with lower-ranking queen only
3rd step	2 higher-ranking queen only
4th step	2 both queens

When investigating a small slam in double-agreement sequences, you are looking to have at least five of the six missing keycards plus at least one queen of the agreed upon suits.

We now consider a **major-major** example.

Opener	Responder	Comments
♠A1073	♠KJ5	
♥A982	♥KQJ63	
♦K2	♦A94	
♣Q7	♣A5	
1♠	2♥	(1) Double Agreement
3♥	3♠ (1)	(2) DRKCB
4♥	4NT (2)	(3) 2 with neither queen
5♥ (3)	6♥ (4)	(4) Q♠ is missing

What if you have a minor – major suit agreement, for example, hearts and diamonds. You may use 4♠ or 4♣ and the Kickback RKCB ask and use 4NT as DRKCB. The responses are similar to the major – major asks.

Scroll Bids (Modified)

With Bergen Raises

When playing Bergen Raises, some use concealed or ambiguous splinter bids. Recall that when opening a major, a jump into the other major indicates a singleton somewhere and four-cards supports with 13+HCP. For example, if one opens one heart, then three spades indicates 13+HCP with four hearts and a singleton somewhere. If one opens one spade, then a response of three hearts shows four spades, 13+HCP, and a singleton somewhere.

To locate the singleton, the opener uses scroll asking bids. Thus, the bidding goes: 1♥ - 3♠, 3NT or 1♠ - 3♥, 3♠. The responses after the 3NT scroll asks are: 4♣, 4♦, 4♠, which shows singletons in either clubs, diamonds, or spades, respectively; and the corresponding responses after bidding 3♠ are: 3NT=♣, 4♣=♦, and 4♦=♥, the suit below the singleton. However, club members have asked me: How do you indicate not a singleton, but a VOID when using the concealed/ambiguous splinter bids?

To show either a singleton or a void, one continues with a scroll bid. Then up-the-line bids are used to show a singleton or VOID and simultaneously provides one with information about keycards for the agreed upon suit. After hearing the response to the asking scroll bids (3NT or 3♠), one uses the next sequential up-the-line bid to determine the nature of the shortage. The responses are: Step 1 (the next cheapest bid) says it is a singleton, and Steps 2-5, the next four bids, indicate that one has a void and simultaneously shows keycards.

To illustrate, suppose we are playing 1430 RKCB. The bidding goes: 1♥ - 3♠, 3NT and one hears the response 4♣. To ask about the nature of the shortage (singleton or void), one uses the next sequential up-the-line bid to ask, bid 4♦. The responses for showing a singleton and/or associated keycards for the major suit (hearts) with a void are:

4♥	club singleton (next cheapest step)
4♠	club void with 1 or 4 keycards (step 2)
4NT	club void with 0 or 3 keycards (step 3)
5♣	club void with 2 keycards w/o the queen (step 4)
5♦	club void with 2 keycards with the queen (step 5)

If you play 0314 RKC, you merely interchange steps 2 and 3 above.

In a similar manner, after hearing 4♦, one would use the up-the-line bid of 4♥ to ask about the nature of the shortage. Now, 4♠ shows a singleton diamond and the keycard steps 2-5 are: 4NT, 5♣, 5♦, and 5♥. After hearing the response 4♠, the up-the-line asking bid is 4NT. Then, 5♣=singleton in spades and the keycard steps (2-5) are: 5♦, 5♥, 5♠, 5NT.

Opening one spade, to show a singleton somewhere with 13+HCP and four-card support is 3♥. After hearing the bid of 3♠, one indicates a singleton with the bids 3NT=♣, 4♣=♦, and 4♥=♠. To ask about the nature of the shortage, one again uses the up-the-line bids: 4♣, 4♦, and 4♠. Again, the next cheapest up-the-line bid indicates a singleton and steps 2-5 are used to show a void and simultaneously keycards for the major suit spades. To illustrate, following the bid of 4♣, the shortage bid is 4♦. The responses follow.

4♥	diamond singleton (next cheapest step)
4♠	diamond void with 1 or 4 keycards (step 2)
4NT	diamond void with 0 or 3 keycards (step 3)
5♣	diamond void with 2 keycards w/o the queen (step 4)
5♦	diamond void with 2 keycards with the queen (step 5)

The responses to the shortage bids of 4♥ and 4♠ follow similarly. **To illustrate how the bid may be used, we consider an example.**

Opener	Responder
♠AQJ762	♠K984
♥3	♥AQ92
♦9872	♦void
♣KQ	♣A7632

Opener	Responder
1♠	3♥ (shortness somewhere)
3♠ (shortage asking bid)	4♣ (singleton/void in diamonds)
4♦ (modified scroll ask)	4NT (void in diamonds with 0/3 keycards)
6♠ (if you have 3, bid 7)	7♠

Using the sequential scroll bids and up-the-bids shortage bids, adapted from bids suggested by the Australian champion George Smolanko for splinter bids, allows one to further investigate the nature of the shortage, a singleton, or a void with information about the keycards in the agreed upon major suit.

Observe that the scroll bids and up-the-line shortage bids may also be used with the Jacoby 2NT* response to a major. If you play that a three-level bid denotes a singleton or a void and a four-level bid shows a strong (not a void) five-card suit, however, now one uses "modified" scroll-like bids to ask about shortage with keycard responses.

After Jacoby 2NT*

When playing Jacoby 2NT after a major suit opening, the three-level bid by responder is alerted and says that one has a singleton or void in the suit bid. **The bid of 2NT* in response to partner's opening bid of one of a major shows at least four trump and 13+ points in support of the major suit. In response to the bid of 2NT*, opener's bid at the three-levels shows a singleton or a void.**

What does responder do next?

With a minimum and no interest based on opener's response, responder usually jumps to game in the agreed suit. All other bids show at least some slam interest. Responder's new suit bids are often cuebids looking for slam.

Are there other options?

Yes, one can use modified scroll bids!

Let's look at two bidding sequences:

(A) 1♠ - 2NT - 3♣/3♦/3♥ which shows a singleton or a void in the suit bid.

(B) 1♥ - 2NT - 3♣/3♦/3♠ which shows a singleton or a void in the suit bid.

To determine whether or not partner has a singleton or a void, one bids as follows.

For sequence (A), one bids: 4♣/4♦/4♥ and for sequence (B), one bids: 4♣/4♦/4♠. A scroll-up bid at the four-levels. Do you have a singleton or a void?

Responses become:

Next cheapest bid shows a singleton
(Step 2) shows 1 or 4 keycards with a void
(Step 3) shows 0 or 3 keycards with a void
(Step 4) shows 2 keycards w/o and a void
(Step 5) shows 2 keycards with the queen and a void

Thus, one is easily able to determine singleton and void with Keycard Blackwood. Let's look at an example:

Opening 1♠ and responding 2NT, suppose partner hears the bid 3♥, which shows a singleton or void in hearts. After hearing the bid of 3♥, one next bids 4♥s to ask whether it is a singleton heart or a void (**note, the bid of four spades is a sign-off**).

The responses follow.

4♠	heart singleton (next cheapest step)
4NT	heart void with 1 or 4 keycards (step 2)
5♣	heart void with 0 or 3 keycards (step 3)
5♦	heart void with 2 keycards w/o the queen (step 4)
5♥	heart void with 2 keycards with the queen (step 5)

Similarly, opening 1♥, the responses after hearing for example 3♠ (a spade singleton or void), and one would bid 4♠.

The responses follow.

5♣	spade singleton (next cheapest step)
5♦	spade void with 1 or 4 keycards (step 2)
5NT	spade void with 0 or 3 keycards (step 3)
5♥	spade void with 2 keycards w/o the queen (step 4)
5♠	spade void with 2 keycards with the queen (step 5

Observe that the asking bids and responses provide all the information required to bid slam or to sign off at the five-level, below slam.

After Jacoby 2NT*, Examples

Previously, I discussed how one may use Scroll Bids with Bergen Raises (when using concealed or ambiguous splinter bids) and after Jacoby 2NT. We now consider two examples of the method when responder bids Jacoby 2NT after a bid of a major.

We consider the Jacoby example found in the July 2009 issue of "Bridge News," available at **www.pitt.edu/~timm**, by clicking on BRIDGE NEWS. "Bridge News" is published monthly by the author.

Dealer East N-S vulnerable

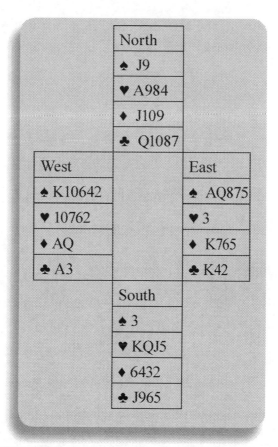

North
♠ J9
♥ A984
♦ J109
♣ Q1087

West		East
♠ K10642		♠ AQ875
♥ 10762		♥ 3
♦ AQ		♦ K765
♣ A3		♣ K42

South
♠ 3
♥ KQJ5
♦ 6432
♣ J965

Suggested Bidding:	West	North	East	South
		1♠	Pass	
	2NT*	Pass	3♥*	Pass
	4♥*	Pass	4♠*	Pass
	4NT	Pass	5♣	Pass
	6♠	Pass	Pass	Pass

West's 2NT is Jacoby 2NT, showing a game-forcing raise with at least four spades.

The bid of 3♥ shows a singleton or void. Hearing shortness, and with four hearts, east bids 4♥ to ask whether or not west has a singleton or a void. The first level bid of 4♠ shows a singleton. Now, west bids 4NT (Keycard Blackwood) to ask about keycards. The response

(5♣) shows one or four; with an ace missing, west signs off in 6♠. We next consider an example with a minor suit void:

	North	
	♠ KJ832	
	♥ A92	
	♦ Void	
	♣ AJ1084	
West		**East**
♠ Q9		♠ 5
♥ 10764		♥ J83
♦ A965		♦ KQJ103
♣ 97		♣ Q653
	South	
	♠ A10764	
	♥ KQ5	
	♦ 872	
	♣ K2	

For this example, the bidding goes:

North	East	South	West
1♠	Pass	2NT*	Pass
3♦*	Pass	4♦*	Pass
4NT*	Pass	5NT	Pass
6♣	Pass	7♠	All pass

Counting high card values and length, north has 13 HCP and 2 length points or 15 Starter points and opens 1♠. South has only 12 Starter points, however, hearing a major suit bid reevaluates to 13 Dummy Points, counting the doubleton, and uses the Jacoby 2NT bid which opener alerts. Opener now bids 3♦ to show the diamond singleton/void. Hearing the shortness bid and with three diamonds, south has slam interest and bids 4♦ to see if north has a singleton or a void, knowing game is ensured. North's response of 4NT (step 3) shows 0 or 3 keycards. South asks about kings by bidding 5NT, 6♣ shows the K♣. North now bids 7♠, a grand slam (with only 25 HCP).

Can you reach the slam without the Modified Scroll Bids? Perhaps. The bidding may go:

North	East	South	West
1♠	Pass	2NT*	Pass
3♦*	Pass	4NT	Pass
6♦	Pass	6♠	Pass
Pass	Pass		

The bid of 4NT is Keycard Blackwood, and 6♦ shows an odd number of keycards with a void in diamonds. Yes, one can now bid 6♠, but observe that getting to the grand slam is difficult.

If you do not play Keycard Blackwood, just Blackwood, Eddie Kantar recommends bidding 5NT with a void and two aces. Again, getting to seven spades is difficult. If south does not bid 4NT, but instead bids four spades, in neither case would one reach the slam.

The use of "Scroll Bids" should enhance the convention card for those who use Bergen Raises (Reverse Bergen Raises or Combined Bergen Raises) playing Two-over One, Standard American, or Precision.

We have reviewed several techniques to investigate slams. Is it worth it? How would you bid the following hand? It came up in a club game last month. North is the dealer. The hand follows. It was played at a club game in the Villages, Florida.

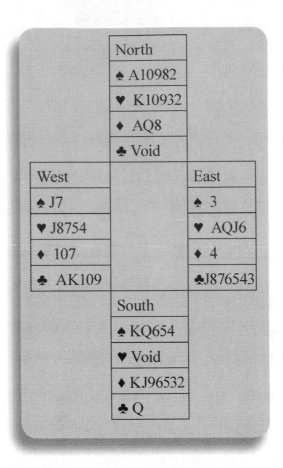

North has 13 HCP and would clearly open 1♠. South has only 11 HCP; however, counting Dummy Points, south has a void and a singleton or at least seven (5-card trump support with a void = 5 points + 2 for singleton) more Dummy Points or 18 Dummy Points. Clearly, in the slam zone. Or, if you count the diamond suit length (3 points) plus 1 more point for the fifth spade, the point count increases to 22; thus, 11 + 22 = 33 or slam values.

What is your bid as south? You have several options: (1) two diamonds as a game force, (2) Jacoby 2NT*, (3) the concealed splinter bid of 3♥*, (4) Swiss bids, etc. Depending on the direction you take, the sequence of bids will differ. We look at several approaches.

Playing Concealed Splinters

North	South	
1♠	3♥*	(singleton or void somewhere)
3♠* (where)	4♥	(hearts)
4♠ (scroll bid)	5♣	(heart void with one keycard)
5♦ (queen ask)	6♠	(yes and extra)
7♠		

Playing Jacoby 2NT

North	South	
1♠	2NT*	(spade raise)
3♣* (singleton/void)	4♣*	(asking bid – singleton or void)
4♠ (void & 1 keycard)	5♥	(cuebid)
6♦ (cuebid)	6♠	
7♠		

Playing EKCB

North	South	
1♠	2♦	(GF)
2♥	2♠	
5♦ (EKCB)	5♠	(one)
6♣ (queen ask)	6♠	
	(yes)	
7♠		

Playing DRKCB with minor + major

North	South	
1♠	2♦	(GF)
2♥	2♠	
3♦	4♠	
4NT (DRKCB)	5NT	(two keycards with higher ranking Q)
6♠	7♥	
7♠		

Cuebidding

North	South	
1♠	2♦	(GF)
2♥	2♠	
3♥	4♦	(cuebid)
5♣ (cuebid)	5♥	(cuebid)
6♦ (cuebid)	6♠	
7♠		

No matter your approach, I hope you all reached the seven spade contract. If you did not get to seven, do not feel badly. Most pairs only bid a small slam, 6♠.

Let's look at a similar hand that was played in the ACBL Summer North American Championships held in Washington, D.C. In this deal, north-south are vulnerable and south is the dealer. How would you bid the hand? Hint: Nothing fancy needed!

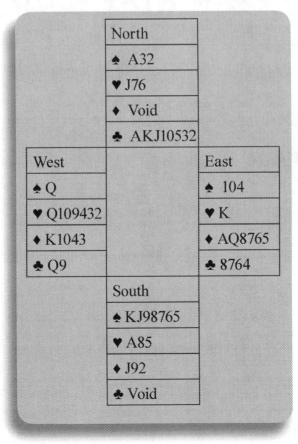

As south, what is your bid? You have only 9 HCP and one of the top three honors with a void. Some may be tempted to open the bidding 3♠; a terrible bid. Do not preempt your partner. Open the bidding 1♠.

South	North
1♠	2♣ (GF)
2♠	4♦ (splinter in support of spades)
4♥ (cuebid)	5♣ (cuebid)
5♠	6♦ (cuebid)
6♠	

Roman Keycard Gerber

When is 4♣ asking for aces (Gerber)? When is 4NT asking for aces (1430 RKCB)? When is 4♣ a cuebid or a splinter? When is 4NT quantitative? What is 4♣ after a transfer? And after Stayman?

These are all questions partnerships must discuss. In general, most partners tend to play Gerber over first and last notrump bids. That means if one opens 1NT or 2NT or if in the bidding sequence one bids 2NT or 3NT, the bid of 4♣ is Gerber.

However, after one agrees on a major, the bid of 4♣ is often played as 1430 Keycard Gerber when not playing Baby Blackwood. Partnerships that do not play Kickback also use 1430 Keycard Blackwood to keep the bidding at a low level in place of 4NT. Still others may not play Gerber over the first and last notrump and instead always use 4♣ as keycard Gerber. The responses to the bids follow 1430 RKCB.

Responses to 4♣ RKCB

4♦	1 or 4 keycards
4♥	0 or 3 keycards
4♠	2 keycards without the queen
4NT	2 keycards with the queen

To show a void with two or four keycards, bid 5NT; with and odd number of keycards, bid the void at the six-level.

Chapter 13 – Interference over 1NT

The Rule of 8

WHEN DEFENDING AGAINST NOTRUMP, interference is typically based upon a weak one- or two-suited hand using some convention like Brozel, Cappelletti, DONT, etc. The problem is how weak is weak? Mel Colchamiro proposed the rule of eight, published in "The Bridge Bulletin," October 2000. The rule follows:

Holding a minimum of six starting points, deduct from the total number of cards in your two longest suits the total number of losing tricks. If the difference is TWO or greater, you should interfere.

If it is less than TWO, do not.

Examples:

♠ AQ943 ♥ K62 ♦ 74 ♣ K86

You have a total of eight cards in your two longest suits. Subtracting seven losers (one in spades plus two each in the other suits) is equal to one. You must NOT interfere even with thirteen starting points.

♠ K7652 ♥ K9532 ♦ 83 ♣ 6

You have a total of ten cards in the long suits. Subtracting seven losers (two each in spades, hearts, diamonds, and one in clubs) is equal to three. You should interfere despite the weakness of your hand, only eight starting points.

The Rule of 2

Mel has another rule that is used in the balancing seat called the Rule of 2.

It is used in the sequence 1NT-Pass-Pass- ?

Should you bid or pass? You should bid only if you have two or more shortness points, regardless of vulnerability, otherwise pass. Let's consider some hands.

♠Q841 ♥ A63 ♦9 ♣ J8642 (yes-bid 2 clubs)

♠A84 ♥ K963 ♦K92 ♣ K86 (no- better to defend -- no shortness points)

♠10643 ♥ Q1095 ♦10 ♣ Q965 (yes- bid 2 clubs)

Interference over Notrump Conventions

In the October 2007 issue of the ACBL "Bridge Bulletin," several experts recommend and discussed systems they play over the bid of a strong 1NT (14/15-17 HCP). Even if you have read the article (also available at www.clairebridge.com/defensevsnt.htm), you still may not have a clear picture about which system is "best."

What system should you play over a weak 1NT (12-14 or 10-12, say), should your approach change playing Match Points vs. IMPS, and should the system change depending upon whether you are in the direct or balancing (pass-out) seat? There is no clear or optimal system for all situations: weak vs. strong NT, Match Points vs. IMPS, direct vs. balancing seat! We consider each in turn, and then recommend an approach. When considering a system to play over the bid of 1NT (weak or strong), the first question you should ask yourself is whether or not a double should be value-showing and penalty-oriented.

Clearly, over a weak NT bid, a double has to show values (14/15+) and be for penalty. Over weak notrumps, if you do not double but defeat the 1NT contract by one or two tricks, you will get an inferior score at Match Points or IMPS. Furthermore, over a weak notrump bid, it is critical to show both majors even if you are 4-4 and have only 10-11 HCP. You may easily compete at the two-levels. Thus, over weak notrumps (Match Points or IMPS), you need a system where a double is for penalty and that is able to show the majors (80 percent of all game bids are played in a major). Finally, over the weak NT bid, it does not matter whether or not the declarer is in the direct or pass-out seat. Hence, it is best to bid your suit, as soon as possible, especially if it is spades! A system designed with these requirements is Mohan. Like most systems designed to interfere over weak notrumps, it is based upon transfers (e.g., Weber). This allows the overcaller a second opportunity to bid, especially with a moderate to good holding. The John Mohan system follows:

Mohan

Double	Penalty
2♣*	shows both majors (4-4 or 5-5)
2♦*	transfer to hearts
2♥*	transfer to spades
2NT*	hearts and a minor

All three-level bids are natural, usually a six-card suit and preemptive.

What if the bid is a strong NT (14/15-17 HCP)? Again, most would agree that a double is value showing and penalty-oriented. We reiterate, NOT ALL AGREE ON THIS. Cappelletti is unwavering in his view. "It must be penalty-oriented. On a particular hand it might not work, but in the long run it's best. Remember that you're 'over' the 1NT opener and that you get to make the opening lead." If you agree, do not adopt any system (IN THE DIRECT SEAT) where a double is not for penalty. Hence, you would not use, for example, DONT, Meckwell, or Brozel. Even though Larry Cohen likes DONT because it allows you to show all one- and two-suit hands without having to bid at the three-levels, the double is NOT for penalty. Furthermore, the system must be able to show the majors at the two-level either directly or indirectly and one usually wants the strong hand on LEAD. If you agree with the above comments and want a system that may be played over either weak or strong notrumps (Match Points or IMPS), it is, in my opinion, the best system is Modified Cappelletti.

Modified CAPPELLETTI

Double: Any double over weak notrump is for penalty. However, over strong notrump bids it may be used for take-out/penalty.

2♣*: Shows a single-suited holding in diamonds OR a two-suited holding in an unspecified major suit and an unspecified minor suit. After a pass by the partner of the notrump bidder, the advancer can bid 2♦, which is forcing for one round. Then the overcaller will either pass or raise with a single-suiter in diamonds if holding stronger values OR bid the major suit if the holding is a two-suiter. Sometimes the overcall holds a six-card club suit and may then bid 3♣ after partner's two diamond bid.

If the overcaller shows the two-suited holding after the 2♦ bid, the advancer can bid 2NT to return to the actual minor suit (clubs or diamonds) or pass if the major suit is preferred.

2♦*: Shows both major suits (as in Cappelletti).

2♥: Shows a single-suited holding in hearts. Partner should pass after a notrump opening by an opponent.

2♠: Shows a single-suited holding in spades. Partner should pass after a notrump opening by an opponent.

2NT*: Shows both minor Suits (5+in each).

WHAT SYSTEM SHOULD YOU ADOPT IN THE PASS-OUT SEAT? Clearly, in the pass-out seat, a double for penalty is not as valuable since the doubler is not on lead against 1NT. In the pass-out seat you should use Modified DONT, also called Meckwell.

Modified DONT (Meckwell)

Double	Shows a 1-suited hand (6+ cards) or both majors.
2♣*	Shows clubs and a major (5-4 or 4-5 or longer).
2♦*	Shows diamonds and a major (5-4 or 4-5 or longer).
2♥	Shows hearts (5+).
2♠	Shows spades (5+).
2NT*	Shows both minor suits (5+in each).

In my opinion, Modified Cappelletti and Modified DONT are my selections for interference over notrump. There have been many methods proposed. I like these methods because they both show the majors immediately and may be used with two-suited or single-suited hands.

In both of the above conventions, 2NT* was used to show the minors. This is sometimes modified to show an equivalent strong notrump hand. Discuss this option with your partner.

When the Opponents Interfere Over 1NT Opening

Lebensohl is a common convention used over weak two bids, reverses, and interference over notrump. However, an even better convention is the Rubinsohl, which uses transfer bids over disruptive interference bids. The basic convention uses the combination of transfers and Lebensohl in a competitive auction aimed at allowing a player to show his distribution with both weak and strong hands. It is similar to the "stolen bid" convention played by many of our members. The method was introduced by Bruce Neill of Australia in an article in The Bridge World in 1983. The concept was based upon the article published in the same magazine by Jeff Rubens, who used the term Rubensohl. However, the method had been previously used in the United States by Ira Rubin, and therefore named Rubinsohl and not Rubensohl. Both names (Rubinsohl and Rubensohl) appear in the bridge literature.

Lebensohl

Lebensohl is used after one opens notrump when the opponents interfere to show game forcing hands immediately. However, the downside of Lebensohl is that you must go through relay bids to find out partner's real suit, and if RHO competes, you might never know that you have a good fit. In today's game, the opponents always seem to use their "toy" to disturb your notrump and the RHO is getting into the action more and more to re-preempt the auction. Ira Rubin and Jeff Rubens thought it was better for partner to announce his suit directly and to show strength later.

The structure of Lebensohl is, briefly:

Double is for penalty.

Two-level bid is to play.

Three-level bid is forcing to game.

Two notrump is artificial, forcing opener to bid three clubs.

An immediate cuebid by responder is Stayman (except after two clubs, double is Stayman).

A direct jump to 3NT denies a stopper.

Two notrump followed by a cuebid of the enemy suit after opener's forced club relay bid is Stayman.

Two notrump followed by three notrump, after a relay to three clubs, shows a stopper and asks opener to play in three notrump.

For example, consider the hand where opener has (♣, ♥, ♦, ♠) xxx AQxx AKxx Kx and the bidding goes: 1NT-2♠-2NT-4♠ and your partner has the hand: x Kxxxxx xx QTxx. You are forced to pass and miss the huge heart fit. Or, you hold xxx Ax Axxx AKxx and the bidding goes 1NT-2♠-2NT-3♠, and partner holds x xxx QJTxxx Qxx, and you guess that he was competing in hearts, so you pass. You missed the five diamond contract. In the first hand, it would be better to transfer to hearts, and in the second, one would want to transfer to diamonds.

To avoid these disasters, one may play Rubinsohl or Rumpelsohl, each part of the Kaplan Sheinwold bidding system.

I do not recommend either; instead, my system of choice is Transfer Lebensohl.

The major disadvantage of Lebensohl is that it results in the play of a hand from the WRONG side; since it is a relay-based system instead of a transfer-based system. This is not the case for Basic Rubinsohl and Transfer Lebensohl.

Transfer Lebensohl

A close cousin to Basic Rubinsohl, and often confused with it, is Transfer Lebensohl. The conventional bids follow. The primary difference in the two systems is in the meaning of the bid of three spades. Primarily, all two-level bids are to play, identical to Lebensohl. However, it may also be played over weak two bids and more as seen below.

Transfer Lebensohl over notrump and weak two bids.

> After (1) 1NT (2X)?
>   (2) (2X) Dbl (P)?
>
>
> (a) X = Diamonds/hearts/spades
>
>   2Y to play where Y is not equal to X
>   2NT: Puppet to 3♣
>   -> Pass /Lower Suit: To play
>   3X cuebid Stayman with stopper GF
>   Over X=H, 3♠=both minors
>   3NT Slammish with stopper
>   3♣: Transfer to diamonds, INV or better *
>   3♦: Transfer to hearts, INV or better *
>   3♥: Transfer to spades, INV or better *
>   * If transfer to opponents -> Stayman w/o stopper

3♠: Transfer to clubs no stopper.

3NT: To play.

4m: Leaping Michaels. 5-5 up.

   (X=M: 4♣=C+oM. 4♦=D+oM.

   X=D: 4♣=C+One major. 4♦=H+S.)

4M: Unbid: NAT. with stopper.

   Jump Cue: Minors. Strong.

4NT: Minors. (Weak if X=M.)

(b) X = Clubs.

Double = Cuebid Stayman w/o stopper.

2Y where Y is not equal to X: To play.

2NT transfer to diamonds no stopper.

   -> 3♦=Accept. 3♣=Decline.

3♣: Stayman with a stopper GF.

3♦: Transfer to hearts, INV or better.

3♥: Transfer to spades, INV or better.

3♠: Transfer to diamonds no stopper.

3NT: To play.

4m: Leaping Michaels.

4M: NAT. with stopper.

It may also be played in the sequence 1X – Dbl -2X?

The best system to play after an overcall of partner's 1NT bid has a long history in the bridge world. For a riveting discussion, one may consult the May/June 1989 issue of "Bridge Today" and the article by Alvin Roth (one of America's foremost bidding theorist) "Doctor Roth's What Do You Bid and Why?" pages 39 – 41. He recommends that one NOT play Lebensohl but use a transfer-based system like either Transfer Lebensohl or Basic Rubinsohl. The Basic Rubinsohl bids follow.

Over a natural 2♠ overcall

2NT	transfer to clubs
3 clubs	transfer to diamonds
3 diamonds	transfer to hearts

3 hearts (transfer into their suit) is Stayman without a stopper

3 spades	transfer to 3NT with a stopper
3NT	natural with a stopper in the bid suit.

Over a natural 2♥ overcall

2 spades is natural and non-forcing

2NT	transfer to clubs
3 clubs	transfer to diamonds

3 diamonds (transfer into their suit) is Stayman without a stopper

3 hearts shows spades with a heart stopper

3 spades shows spades without a stopper in hearts

3NT	natural with a stopper in the bid suit.

If the opponents overcall a natural minor, the treatment is as follows. Two-level bids are natural and non-forcing. With the overcall 2♦, 2NT shows clubs as usual, but 3♣ is Stayman for both majors and asks if partner has a diamond stopper. If no major or stopper, one simply accepts the transfer. Jumps in the majors are natural and forcing. The bids of 3♦/3♥ are transfers. But, 3♠ is partnership defined as most use it to show a club bust (Minor Suit Stayman). A bid of 3NT shows a stopper in diamonds.

With a 2♣ (natural or not) overcall, a double is Stayman without a club stopper and two-level bids are natural and competitive. 2NT is generally defined as Stayman with a club stopper. A jump to a three-level bid is a transfer and forcing.

With so many "toys" being used over 1NT, Rubinsohl and Transfer Lebensohl have a distinct advantage over Lebensohl since you know your suit early and it ignores the RHO getting into the act. In both systems, a double is not for penalty but for takeout.

Chapter 14 – Comments 2/1 and Precision

ANY BIDDING SYSTEM, WHETHER it is 2/1 Game Force or Precision in Match Point play, must be able to get to the correct contract (suit or notrump) and to the correct level (partial, game, or slam). In addition, you cannot win if you go against the field. Your goal is always to get a positive score. Any positive score will be better than all those pairs that go negative. In Precision, your opening bid is usually always the same; it does not depend upon seat location. Never "stretch" your bid. After reading this book, should you play 2/1 Game Force or Precision? We consider a few hands.

(1)	Opener	♠K2	♥108	♦AKJ7	♣QJ987
	Responder	♠A654	♥Q765	♦86	♣K102

Bidding Sequence for Precision: 1♦* - 1♥ - 2♣ - pass

Bidding Sequence for 2/1: 1♦ - 1NT – pass

Playing the hand, one makes four clubs for a score of 130 while the 2/1 Game Force player only makes 2NT for a score of 120.

(2)	Opener	♠AK2	♥KQJ108	♦AQJ4	♣7
	Responder	♠1054	♥A65	♦K1052	♣KQ2

Playing Precision, the bidding would go:

Opener	Partner
1♣*	1♠* (transfer to notrump, balanced with 8 – 13 HCP)
1NT	2♥ (5 hearts)
3♦	4♦
4♥	4♠ 1430 keycard based upon diamonds
5♥ (2 w Q)	6♦

Playing 2/1, the bidding may go:

1♥	3♦ (10 -12 HCP and 3 hearts)
4♠ (RKCB)	5♣ (2 keycards)
6♥	

The primary advantage of Precision over 2/1 is that the bids are more precise, helping you to easily determine whether you should be in a partial contract, game, or slam. The bids are structured and well defined with specific point ranges. While there are many similarities between Precision and 2/1 when opening one of a major, it is sufficiently different, for most other bids, that many players in the United States who play 2/1 do not understand the bidding structure of Precision. Playing in team games and Match Points events, this can be a clear advantage.

Asking Bids after a Preempt

How many times has your partner opened at the three-level and you find yourself with a very good hand? What do you bid? Often, neither Blackwell nor cuebids help. To consider a specific example, suppose you pick up the hand:

♠AQ4 ♥AKQ654 ♦ A10 ♣ 84

Following, your partner opens three spades. What do you bid? The problem revolves around what your partner has in the club suit.

Consider the following three OPENING hands.

1. ♠KJ109765 ♥32 ♦K76 ♣2
2. ♠KJ109763 ♥32 ♦K9 ♣J10
3. ♠KJ109543 ♥32 ♦87 ♣A2

Opposite hand 1, six spades is a lay down. With the second hand, six cannot be made because of the two club losers. And, with the third hand, seven is a lay down. The same problem occurs when your partner opened four spades.

With hand 3, Blackwood solves the problem, but what about hands 1 and 2? The solution is to play ASKING BIDS whenever one opens at the three-/four-level.

For a three-level bid, any JUMP response in a suit is an asking bid in that suit.

Thus, after 3♠ followed by 5♣ asks, what do you have in clubs?

After 3♦ followed by 4♥ asks, what do you have in hearts?

Following a FOUR-level bid, any five-level bid becomes an asking bid.

After 4♥ the bid of 5♦ asks, what do you have in diamonds?

After 4♠, the bid of 5♣ asks about clubs.

These bids do not interfere with normal bidding procedures because a new suit in response to a preemptive bid is forcing so that responder need not jump to game. Thus, the jump bid may be used more profitably. When opening at the four-levels, opener should have a very powerful suit and responder is not likely to have a better one. Hence, responder is more likely to make an asking bid.

Responses to Asking Bids

Let's consider an example with the sequence: 3♠ followed by 5♣, what do you have in clubs?

Responses to asking bids ALWAYS start with the next suit.

First Step – 2 or more quick losers, xx, xxx, xxxx

Second Step – singleton

Nearest notrump regardless of step = king

Fourth Step – ace

Fifth Step – AK or AQ.

Sixth Step - Void

> (1) Opener's Hand: ♠K4 ♥65 ♦AJ109432 ♣43
>
> Responder's Hand: ♠87 ♥AKQJ109 ♦K4 ♣AKQ.

The bidding goes, 3♦ followed by 4♠. What do you have in spades? The bid of 4NT shows a KING, closest NT, and responder bids 6NT to protect the king. Notice that in this case, the first step is notrump, showing the king. With two or three small spades, opener would have responded 5♣ to the 4♠ asking bid.

> (2) Opener's Hand: ♠AKJ98765 ♥32 ♦2 ♣54
>
> Responder's Hand: ♠Q104 ♥J7 ♦AKQJ ♣AKJ10.

The bidding goes, 4♠ followed by 5♥. What do you have in hearts? Opener bids 5♠, first step, to show two or more quick losers in hearts. Responder passes.

Always discuss asking bids with your partner.

Because I have tried to structure this book around the 2/1 Game Force System, I hope those who play 2/1 may easily convert to the Precision Simplified.

Chapter 15 – Weak Notrump Option

Overview

MANY PRECISION PARTNERSHIPS EMPLOY the weak notrump often called Kamikaze notrump. This option allows players to open balanced 10 HCP hands. However, the risk of opening these hands vulnerable is great. Hence it is often replaced by what is called chicken notrump. With this option, one opens 1NT with 10-12 HCP non-vulnerable and 13-15 when vulnerable.

Weak Hands (10-12)

With a weak 1NT opening (10-12), one should have a balanced hand and one of the following distributions: 4-3-3-3, 5-3-3-2, or 4-4-3-2 with length in a minor or a weak non-biddable major. Let's consider a few examples:

(1) ♠ KJ87 ♥ 10853 ♦ AK3 ♣ J3	(2) ♠ KJ7 ♥ 93 ♦ Q1063 ♣ AQ84	(3) ♠ 75 ♥ AJ2 ♦ A93 ♣ K10875

(4) ♠ KJ7 ♥ J8753 ♦ A106 ♣ Q5	(5) ♠ AJ72 ♥ 104 ♦ J84 ♣ KQJ5	(6) ♠ 632 ♥ AQ105 ♦ AQ109 ♣ J6

Responder with a balanced hand must take into account that game is possible only if he has 13+ HCP. We review some bids after a weak NT opener.

2♣	non-forcing Stayman	10-12 HCP
2♦	forcing Stayman	13+ HCP
2♥/2♠	to play	0-8 HCP
3♣/3♦/3♥/3♠	6+ card suit	9-11 HCP

Opener bids 2♦/2NT with no four-card major, two of a major with four, where 2♥ may imply both.

After 1NT-2♣-2♦

Pass	Garbage Stayman
2♥, 2♠	to play (2♣)/invitational (2♦)
2NT	invitational
3m	5+ card suit, game forcing, slam oriented. By a passed hand it is invitational with a 4-card major and 5+ cards in the minor
3M	Smolen
4♣	Gerber
4♦, 4♥	Delayed Texas transfer, 6+ in the majors, no slam interest/very strong hand with a void
4NT, 5NT	Quantitative
5M	GSF

After 1NT-2♣-2M:

2NT	invitational
3m	5+ card suit, game forcing, slam oriented. By a passed hand it is invitational with a 4-card major and 5+ cards in the minor.
3M	Invitational

Sets M as trump suit, and responder may be planning to RKCB in M in his next bid (kickback/1430).

4m	void, fit in M, slam interest
4NT, 5NT	Quantitative

5M	GSF
5m, 6X	Signoff

After 1NT opening,

2♥, 2♠	to play
2NT	invitational
3♣, 3♦, 3♥, 3♠	natural and invitational

Interference with weak NT is common.

After double, 1NT-double, the following scheme may be used.

Redouble	shows clubs
2-level bids	Transfers and Signoff
Pass	Opener is asked to show a 5-card minor or to redouble with none
	After opener redoubles, responder starts bidding suits up-the-line.
2NT	Two-suited monster
3X	Weak hand 7+ card suit
3NT	Solid 7+ card minor, nothing else outside, opener is expected to bid 4 clubs without reasonable stoppers

After the auction: 1NT-p-p-X-p-p:

Redouble	5-card minor, opener relays to 2 clubs
2♣, 2♦, 2♠	Lower of 2 4-card suits

With the auction 1NT-2X, a natural or artificial bid, you can play Lebensohl, Rubinsohl, Rumpelsohl (a combination of Lebensohl and Rubinsohl), or Transfer Lebensohl.

After the auction 1NT-p-2♣-2X

Opener rarely bids. A double would be for penalties. 2M shows a good fitting maximum [4-4-2-3] hand when X=♦, otherwise it shows a maximum hand with two small cards in X.

After the auction 1NT-p-2♣-X

In general, the opener will indicate whether he should be playing in 2♣-doubled. Therefore, pass shows a good four-card suit allowing opener to redouble for business, redouble shows a five-card suit.

After the auction 1NT-p-2♦-X and 1NT-p-2♥-X

Responses are unchanged except that opener must pass with two cards in partner's suit. Redouble is natural showing a fair 4+card suit and willing to play the redoubled contract.

After the auction 1NT-p-p-2X

Opener's double is for takeout, showing exactly xx in opponents' suit. Responder's double is penalty-oriented: opener must take out with xx in the opponents' suit or other poor defensive hand.

As responder, it denies a 5+card major, he may compete on the two-level showing his cheapest four-card suit, or with 2NT showing both minors (or if X=♠, any take-out).

The primary advantage of playing a weak NT is its preemptive value. Let's consider an example.

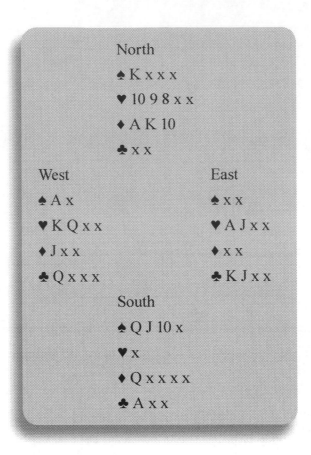

Playing a weak NT, west opens 1NT. Neither north nor south can afford to overcall at the two-level; so, the contract is played at 1NT. If, however, you opened the west hand one diamond, north might double and the spade game by north-south would be reached. While the east-west pair cannot make 1NT, the contract should be down two for a north-south score of 200. This is clearly better than the game score of 620. However, if north leads the ♥10, with no information to guide the lead, the contract was made!

Weak Notrump Runouts

When the opponents make a penalty double of your weak 1NT opening bid, your side can be at serious risk of being set and going for a very large penalty; this is particularly the case with the 10-12 HCP weak notrump opening. While we discussed the Meckwell runout bids in Chapter 7, there are other options:

Exit Transfer Notrump Runouts

If the opponents have doubled your partner's 1NT opening bid, Exit Transfer Notrump Runouts provide you with a way to try to escape the penalty with as little damage as possible. Exit Transfers additionally have the benefit of allowing the notrump opener to declare most two-level contracts, "right-siding" them.

Playing Exit Transfers after the auction has gone 1NT-Double, Redouble is a transfer to 2♣ and shows 5+ clubs, 2♣ is a transfer to diamonds and shows 5+ diamonds, 2♦ is a transfer to hearts and shows 5+ hearts, and 2♥ is a transfer to spades and shows 5+ spades. If you have a two-suited hand, you should pass; your pass forces partner to redouble, then with a hand well suited to play 1NT redoubled you can pass or else you can describe your two-suited hand by bidding 2♣ to show clubs and a higher-ranking suit, 2♦ to show diamonds and a major and 2♥ to show both majors.

For the purposes of runout bids, a hand is two-suited if it is 4-4 or better, and it is single-suited if it contains a six-card or longer suit or a five-card suit without another four-card suit. If 4-3-3-3, it is usually best to pretend the hand is two-suited.

Helvic Notrump Runouts

Helvic Notrump Runouts is a convention popular in England. Part of the reason for the popularity of this convention is that the Standard English/ACOL system contains a weak notrump opening bid, which is significantly more susceptible to penalty doubles.

If the opponents have doubled your partner's 1NT opening bid, Helvic Notrump Runouts provide you with a way to try to escape the penalty with as little damage as possible. Playing Helvic, you can either show a single-suited hand by redoubling or show a two-suited hand by bidding at the two-level. A 2♣ bid shows clubs and diamonds, a 2♦ bid shows diamonds and hearts, a 2♥ bid shows hearts and spades, and a 2♠ bid shows spades and clubs. If you redouble, partner will bid 2♣ as a pass-or-correct bid. And finally, if you wish to play in 1NT despite the double, or if you have a two-suited hand with non-touching suits, you should pass. Your pass forces partner to redouble so you can play 1NT redoubled, or so you can bid 2♣ to show clubs and hearts or 2♦ to show diamonds and spades. For the purposes of runout bids, a hand is two-suited if it is 4-4 or better, and it is single-suited if it contains a six-card or longer suit or a five-card suit without another four-card suit. If 4-3-3-3, it is usually best to pretend the hand is two-suited.

Multi-suit weak two bids

The opening bids of 2♦/2♥/2♠ usually show a hand with 6-10 HCP and a six-card suit. Is there a better bidding strategy?

Yes, how about the multi-suit weak two bids.

The bids are defined:

2♦	Single heart suit or two suits: Clubs and spades or clubs and diamonds
2♥	Single spade suit or two suits: Hearts and clubs or hearts and diamonds
2♠	Single club suit or two suits: Spades and diamonds or spades and hearts

Note that the single-suited hands are the next level suit (diamonds implies hearts, hearts implies spades and spades implies clubs), and transfer like bids. Hence, responder bids the next suit up-the-line to play and opener passes if the hand is single-suited. If opener has a two-suited hand, he refuses the two-level bids and bids three clubs (after 2♦-2♥-3♣) or three diamonds (after 2♥-2♠-3♦ or 2♠-3♣-3♦), the lower ranking suit of a two-suited hand.

With game interest, responder does not use the relay bids of hearts, spades, and clubs but instead bids 2NT.

Now, opener bids his suit if single-suited (hearts, spades, or clubs) at the three-level. If two- suited, he again bids three clubs or three diamonds, the lower ranking suit, with minimal values (5-7 HCP).

With 8-10 HCP, opener bids 3NT if single-suited or the higher ranking suit at the three-level if holding a two-suited hand. For example, the bids would be: after 2♦-2NT-3♠, after 2♥-2NT-3♥, and after 2♠ -2NT -3♠.

Let's look at two examples.

(1)   Opener: ♠ 6 ♥ A Q 8 7 6 5 ♦ 6 5 3   ♣ 10 7 6

               Responder: ♠ A Q 7 8 ♥ J 10 ♦ J 10 4 ♣ A 2

In (1), opener bids 2♦*. Responder with only 12 HCP, bids 2♥, and opener would pass.

(2)   Opener: ♠ 6 ♥ A Q 8 7 6 5 ♦ 6 5 3 ♣ 10 7 6

               Responder: ♠ A K J 8 ♥ K J 10 9 ♦ A 10 4 ♣ 4 2

In (2), after opener's bid of 2♦*, responder bids 2NT. With only 6 HCP, opener bids 3♥ to show a minimal single-suited hand. Responder bids 4♥; however, with fewer points and no fit responder could pass.

Some may feel that the multi-suit weak two bidding structure defined above is too complicated. Because the bids are weak, the structure must be involved to differentiate between invitational hands and game going hands.

If one increases the value of "weak" bids to hands with more points, say 10 -12 HCP, the bidding structure may be greatly simplified; however, you have now given up weak two bids. With weak bids increased in value, one may perhaps adopt the following bidding structure. Instead of using transfer bids, one may define a structure of bids as follows:

2♦	diamonds or diamonds and a lower ranking suit
2♥	hearts or hearts and a lower ranking suit
2♠	spades or spades and a lower ranking suit.

With a weak hand, responder may pass; there is no relay involved. With game interest, responder bids 2NT. Now the bid of 2NT becomes an asking bid. What is your second suit if two-suited?

Now having a second suit, you would rebid your suit at the three-level; however, with a two-suited hand, you would bid your lower ranking suit.

The revised bidding structure of 10-12 HCP is not arbitrary; it is identical to opening a weak notrump. Thus, if you play weak notrumps, you might want to also consider the two-suited/single-suited "weak" bids. Just a thought!

Let's look at two examples.

(1) ♠ 83 ♥ K J 10 9 8 ♦ J   ♣ A Q 10 9 8

(2) ♠ J 10 9 4 ♥ Q J 10 7 ♦ J 10 3 ♣ A Q 10

Hand (1) has only 11 HCP, but you are 5-5 in hearts and clubs. Open the bidding 2♥. Hand (2) also has 11 HCP, however, it is balanced. Playing weak notrumps, open the hand 1NT.

If you adopt the weak notrump bid and the weak two bids with 10-12 HCP, consider the following bidding structure vulnerable or non-vulnerable.

10-12	open the bidding 1NT
13 -15	open 1♣, rebid 1NT
16-17	open 1♦, rebid 1NT
18-19	open one of a suit, rebid 2NT
20-12	open the bidding 2NT

Suggestion: It is always advisable to reevaluate your bidding agreements and perhaps try a new one.

Chapter 16 – System Summary

Basic Opening bids

1♣*	Artificial 16+ HCP --- MUST ALERT
1♦*	11-15 HCP may be short usually 2+ ♦, but may be only one- MUST ALERT (May have a 4-card major)
1♥/1♠	11-15 HCP 5+ Majors with Combined Bergen Bidding Structure (as in 2/1 Game Force)
1NT	13-15 HCP and no 5-card Major with a balanced hand (as in 2/1 Game Force with Double-Barrel Stayman)
2♣*	11-15 HCP 6+ Clubs (may have a 4-card major) - MUST ALERT
2♦*	11-15 HCP 4=4-4-1/ 4=4-0-4 (Mini-Roman Modified - MUST ALERT)
2♥/2♠	5-10 HCP 6+ Cards (Weak 2-bids Vulnerable with Ogust)
2NT*	5-5 in the minors 4-8 HCP (NV) and 8-12 HCP (Vulnerable)
3X	5-10 must have 2/3 of top 3 Honors in the Bid Suit Vulnerable and 1 if Non- vulnerable
3NT*	GAMBLING solid 7+ minor suits (AKQJxxx)

* Indicates forcing bids and alerts

Responses to 1♣* Opening

Responses to 1♣* OPENING (16+ HCP balanced hand, 17 + HCP for an unbalanced hand and a major with 4+ cards)

(1) Negative: 1♦* 0-7 HCP

Opener Rebids after 1♦*:

Non-forcing bids: 1♠/2♣/2♦ (minimum unbalanced hands with 5/6-card suits, 16-19 HCP).

1♥* relay responder must respond 1♠*

Opener Rebids after 1♥*

1NT 20-21 HCP balanced may have a 5-card major

2♣	5+ hearts, 4+ clubs, non-forcing
2♦	5+hearts, 4+ diamonds, non-forcing
2♥	5+ heart suit, no extras
2♠	5+hearts, 4+ spades, non-forcing

2NT 24-25 HCP balanced.

3♣/3♦	Forcing, possibly 5-5 in hearts and the suit bid (clubs/diamonds)
3♥	six-card suit, invitational over the one diamond response
3♠	5+ hearts, 4+ spades with extras
3NT	to play
4♣	6 clubs, 5 diamonds, forcing
4♦	6 diamonds, 6 clubs, forcing
4♥	to play
4NT	RKCB

Exceptions -- Do not relay hearts to spades if the following conditions apply.
After 1♥* responder bids:

1NT	5-5 or better in the majors, very weak (0-4 HCP)
2♣/2♦/2♥/2♠	modest 6+ card suit, very weak
2NT	5-5 or better in the minors, very weak (0-4 HCP)
3♣/3♦/3♥/3♠	modest 7+ card suit, very weak

After 2♥* responder bids:

| 2NT | 2-suited 5-5 or better, extremely weak (0-2) |
| 3♣/3♦/3♥/3♠ | modest 7+ card suit, extremely weak |

1NT* 16-19 HCP Balanced May have a 5-card Major

Partner	Responses
Pass	0-6 HCP
2♣	6-7 HCP, Stayman
2♦/2♥	Jacoby Transfer
2NT	7HCP, inviting 3NT

2♠ without relay shows 5- spades and 22+HCP -- equivalent of Standard bidders 2♣ (no-relay)

| 4♠ by responder is to play (7 or less HCP) after one diamond response |
| With a positive response of 1 club, bids follow 2/1 structure |

2♥* relay responder must bid 2♠*

Opener Bids and Corresponding Partner Rebids

2NT 26-27 HCP balanced hand may have a 4-card major

New Suit	shows a king
3NT	0-4 HCP, denies a king
4NT	5-7 HCP, invite slam

3♥ - 5/6+hearts -- equivalent of 2/1 bidders 2♣ 22+ HCP (forcing)

3NT	0-4 HCP, minimum and no support
4♥	0-4 HCP, minimum and 2-card support

3♣/3♦ - unbalanced very strong 7+ minor hand (game force, 22+HCP)

New suit	shows king or void
3NT	shows king or void
Raise to game	denies king, singleton, or void

4♣/4♦------ 6-5 clubs-diamonds/6-5 diamonds-clubs 22+ HCP

New suit	shows or void
4NT	no king or void
Raise to game	denies king, singleton, or void

2NT* 22-23 HCP balanced may have 5-card major (no relay bid)

Partner Responses

Pass	0-2 HCP

Other bids same as 2/1 (e.g., 3♠ is minor suit Stayman)

3NT 28+ HCP balanced may have a five-card major

Partner Rebids

0-3 HCP   pass or 4-level bids are transfers

4-7 HCP and balanced   bid 5NT invite slam

---

(2) Transfers to MAJORS Positive Bids 8+ HCP:

1♥#   **5+spades opener bids 1♠,**
2♦#   **5+ hearts opener bids 2♥,**
1♠#   **balanced hand (8-13 HCP and may have a 5-card minor) opener bids 1NT**

Opener's Responses with Balanced Hands

1NT	16-19 HCP
2NT	20-21 HCP
3NT	22-23 HCP
4NT	24+ HCP (Blackwood)

 # announced as a transfer

The bid of 2♣* shows long minor and the bid of 1NT* by responder ensure 4-4 in the majors (with 8 – 13 HCP) details (3) and (4) below.

Opener (Only accepts Transfer if he has a fit by bidding 1♠/2♥ with at least two-card support + Honor or three-card support). After the bid of 1NT, Stayman is used.

3♥/3♠	Balanced minimum transfer accepts exactly 16HCP
4♥/4♠	To play, accept bids with 17 HCP

Responder uses (Gamma) control bids to show length after opener ACCEPTS showing 18+ HCP.

2/3♣* by responder says I have 5
2/3♦* by responder says I have 6
2/3♥* by responder says I have 7

When responder bids two clubs showing only five-cards in the accepted major, opener may bid two diamonds (the next step) to ask about NT. Responder will bid a suit when at the two-level to show a stopper. 2NT shows stoppers in both minors. A rebid of the five-card major at the two-level shows no stoppers.

Next level bids of MAJOR by Opener at the 2/3 level after Gamma bids are Trump Asking Bids (TAB) used to investigate suit quality.

Responses to TAB follow (NT is not used as a step):

1st step	3/4♣* no Honors in agreed major
2nd step	3/4♦* 1 top Honor
3rd step	3/4♥* 2 top Honors
4th step	3/4♠* 3 top Honors

An important adjunct to Gamma length bids (when one has 6/7 trump) or the TAB is a new suit (Epsilon) Shortness Asking Bids (SAB) which is initiated by bidding the SUIT! Note that this is used for the investigation of SLAM in a suit and NOT Notrump.

Responses to SAB are:

1st step no shortness

2nd step singleton

3rd step void

NT is not used as a step "reserved for RKCB"

NON-TRANSFER BIDS by OPENER ------- 5+card suit of his own denying a fit in the transfer major. Or one may bid 1NT showing balanced hand with 16-19 HCP. Responding with Balanced Hands and not major suit fit.

1/2NT*	16-19 HCP
2/3NT*	20-21 HCP
3/4NT*	22-23 HCP
4/5NT	24+ HCP (Blackwood)

(3) 1NT* 8 – 13 HCP Two 4-card Majors

2♣/2♦	16+ HCP, 5+ card suit and no major fit
2♥/2♠	shows 3-card support for the major with ruffing values
2NT	Forcing (16+ HCP) asking partner to bid minor suit stoppers
	Responder (Partner) Rebids
	Bid minor stopper suit (Qxx)
	Both minors stopped, bid 3NT
	None – Bid best major
3♣/3♦	16+ HCP, 6+ card suit and no major fit
3♥/3♠	Invitational to game in the major with fit (16+ HCP)
3NT	16 + HCP and usually 2-cards support in major
4♥/4♠	Sign-off
4NT	Blackwood Ace Asking

(4) 2♣* 8+ HCP 6-cards in a Minor with 2 of top 3 honors

Opener Rebids (after 1♣* - 2♣*) – Summary

2♥/2♠	Shows a 5-card major suit

Partner Rebids
Raise major with support or bid minor

2NT	Asking partner for Minor (bid it)

Partner **Rebids**
3NT	Sign-off
4♣*/4♦ *	Trump Asking Bid (TAB)
	0 Bid Game
	1-2 Bid Slam
	3 Bid Grand Slam

3NT	No interest in slam or the minor
4NT	Blackwood Ace Asking

(5) 2♥/2♠ 4-6 HCP 6+card (Weak Jump Shift)

Opener Rebids

Pass	Game unlikely
4♥/4♠/3NT	20+ HCP
New suit	5+ cards without support for the majors

Partners Rebids

Raise	3+ support (or Qx)
Rebid ♥/♠	minimum no support
Cuebid under 3NT	singleton or void

3♥/3♠	Minimal hand with support (16-18 HCP)

Partners Rebids

Pass or bid game

2NT	Ogust
3NT	Natural
4NT	RKCB

(6) 2NT* 14+HCP, balanced no 5-card major (May not stop short of 4NT)

Opener Rebids

3♦/3♥/3♠	Natural bids
3♣	Baron asking bid
	Partner Bids
	Bid 4-card suits up-the-line
	3NT show clubs
4NT	Quantitative

(7) 3♣* 1-4-4-4/4-4-4-1 Black Singleton Lacking 4 controls (8 – 13 HCP)

Opener Rebids after 3♣

3♦*	Where is the singleton?		
		3♥*	club singleton
		3♠*	spade singleton
3NT	to play		
4♥/4♠	to play		
4NT	Blackwood ace asking		

Cuebid by opener of singleton (4♣*/4♠*) is the CAB

1st step 0-2 (at most 1 ace or 2 kings)

2nd step 3 (ace and king)

3rd step 4 (2 aces)

(8) 3♦* 4-1-4-4/4-4-1-4 Red Singleton Lacking 4 controls (8-13 HCP)

> **Rebids after 3♦**
>
> **3♥*** Where is singleton?
>
>   **3♠***   diamond singleton
>   3NT*   heart singleton
>
> **4♥/4♠** to play
> 4NT   Blackwood ace asking
>
> Cuebid by opener of singleton (4♦*/4♥*) is the CAB
>
>   1st step 0-2 (at most 1 ace or 2 kings)
>   2nd step 3 (ace and king)
>   3rd step 4 (2 aces)

(9)   (Submarine Strong Singleton Responses after 1♣ bids)

> **3♥***   specifically 1-4-4-4 with 4+ controls, usually 14+ HCP
> **3NT***   specifically 4-4-4-1 with 4+ controls, usually 14+HCP
> **4♣***   specifically 4-4-1-4 with 4+ controls, usually 14+HCP
> **4♦***   specifically 4-1-4-4 with 4+ controls, usually 14+HCP

Next level bids BY OPENER are CAB (3♠*, 4♣*, 4♦* and 4♥*, respectively)
The responses to the CAB are:

     1st step -- 4 controls (2 aces or ace and 2 kings)
     2nd step --5 controls (2 aces and 1 king/ ace + 3 kings)
     3rd step --6 controls (3 aces/ 2 aces and 2 kings)

(10) 3♠* a solid 7+ card suit (AKQJxxx), 14 + HCP with or without side controls

Opener Rebids (with minimal 16 – 17 HCP)

3NT   to play

4♥/4♠   natural showing at least 5-cards with no slam interest

Opener bids with 18+ HCP (if he knows the suit)

4♣*   CAB - Asks about outside suit controls

Reponses to CAB

4♦*   no outside controls

4♥*   outside king

4♠*   outside ace or 2 kings

4NT*   ace/2-3 kings

Opener bids with 18 + HCP (if suit is unknown)

4♦*   asking for suit

Responses to suit ask

4♥*/4♠*/5♣*   hearts, spades, clubs

4NT*   diamonds

Opener may also bid 4NT which is Blackwood

Responses to 1M Opening

Responses to 1M Opening (Open 1♥/1♠ with 11-15 HCP) -- Same as 2/1, Combined Bergen

Responses to 1NT Opening

Responses to 1NT (13-15 HCP)

2♣	NF Stayman	10-12 HCP
2♦	Forcing Stayman	13+HCP
2♥/2♠	to PLAY	0-8 HCP
3♣/3♦/3♥/3♠	6-card suit with 2 of top 3 honors	9-11 HCP

Responses to 2M Opening

Responses to 2♥/ 2♠ (Open 5-10 HCP, 6+ suit --- occ. 5) - Same as 2/1

The weak major two-level bid is a "normal" weak two and typically shows between 5-10 points and at least a six-card suit. The optimum hand for a weak 2 has most of its points in the long suit although it is recognized that this is not always possible and sometimes (particularly third hand at favorable vulnerability) you have to go with what you've got.

Responses to 2♣* Opening

Responses to 2♣ Opening (Open 11-15 HCP, 6+ clubs or 6 clubs and 4 cards major, must have two of the top three honors --- 5+ in third seat.

Partner responses

2♦*   11+ HCP, conventional and forcing for one round

Opener Rebids

2♥	11-13 HCP, 4-card ♥ suit
2♠	11-13 HCP, 4-card ♠ suit
2NT	11-13 HCP, 6-3-2-2 BAL hand, 6-card club suit with a major stopper

Partner Rebid

3♦*	requests opener to clarify stoppers

Opener Bids

3♥*	♥ stopper
3♠*	♠ stopper
3NT	♥ and ♠ stoppers

3♣	14-15 HCP non-forcing and unbalanced hand (1-3-3-6)
3♥	14-15 HCP, 5+card ♥ suit
3♠	14-15 HCP, relay back to ♣'s, solid club suit AKJ109x allows responder to bid 3NT
3NT	14-15 HCP, 5+spades and 6+ clubs

2♥/2♠	Natural with 5+cards, 8-10 HCP
2NT	Natural 10-12 HCP
3♣	Preemptive raise not forward going
3♦/3♥/3♠	6+ card suit, 12 HCP opener may pass, raise, or bid 3NT
4♣	Invitational to game in clubs
4♥/4♠	Natural and to play
4♦	RKCB for clubs

With interference

Negative double through 3♠	
Redouble	10+ HCP
Cuebid	13+ HCP

Responses to 2♦* Opening (Modified Mini-Roman)

Responses to 2♦* Opening (11-15 HCP) Shows a hand with one of the following distributions (4=4-4-1, 4=4-5-0).

Partner Response to 2♦*

2♥/2♠   3+ card support 0-12 HCP

2NT*   13+ HCP (asks partner to bid singleton)

     Opener Rebids
     3♣*/3♦* 4=4=4=1/4=4=1=4 singleton in bid suit
     4♣*/4♦* 4=4=5=0/4=4=0=5 void in bid suit
     Partner sets the contract or bids 4NT (Blackwood)

3♣/3♦   13+ HCP with own 5-card suit

     Opener Rebids
     Pass   11 HCP
     3NT   12+ HCP denies support for the minor
     Bidding other minor at the 4-level is an asking bid - bid best major

3♥/3♠   shows 13+ HCP and 4+ cards in major
3NT   16+ HCP and support for 1 major
4♣*/4♦*   splinter bid with singleton and support for 1 major
5♣*/5♦*   void in bid suit with support for 1 major

With interference
     Negative double through 3♠
     Redouble   10+ HCP
     Cuebid   13+ HCP

Responses to 1♦* Opening

Responses to 1♦* Opening (11-15 HCP diamonds may be short) strong Jump Shifts

1♥/1♠ 4+ cards in suit with 6+ HCP (to show weak hand rebid majors since using strong jump shifts)

1NT	8-10 HCP, balanced hand
2NT	11- 12 HCP, balanced hand
3NT	13-15 HCP, balanced hand
2♣	13+ HCP forcing one round
2♦*	13+ HCP with 6+ diamonds forcing one round
2♥/2♠	16+ HCP strong jump shift in Major 5+ cards, game force
3♣*	10-12 HCP, 6+ diamonds (Crisscross)
3♦*	less than 10 HCP, weak, preemptive raise 6+♦
3♥/3♠	Splinter bid in support of diamonds (slam interest 16+)
4♣	Splinter bid in support of diamonds (slam interest 16+)
4♦	Minorwood 1430 Keycard for diamonds
4♥/4♠	Single-suited hand to play

Getting to notrump

After an inverted minor raise 1♦* - pass - 2♦* (13+ HCP)

1. Show major suit stoppers 2♥ or 2♠, bid up-the-line. No extra values
2. Bid **2NT** with a minimum and both majors are stopped
3. Bid **3♣** to show club stopper, neither hearts of spades stopped
4. Bid **3♦** with a minimum without major stoppers
5. Bid **3♥** or **3NT**, showing ♥ stopped, over **2♠** with minimum values

After a weak raise 1♦* - pass - 3♦* (less than 10 HCP)

a. Pass with all minimum and almost all intermediate sized hands
b. A new suit is forcing one round and shows a very strong hand
c. **3NT** is to play regardless what partner had for his preemptive raise
d. **4 of the minor** is invitational (may be used as RKC Blackwood)

Note: After **1♦*-2♦***, you can bid major stoppers *out of order* to show club shortness below **3NT**. Opener bids **2♠** and then, over a **2NT** or **3♦** response, bids **3♥**. This shows club shortness and enough values for game while still allowing **3NT** to be bid by par.

When they double

If the bidding goes: 1♦* - double; bid as follows:

REDOUBLE	shows 5+ hearts	asks partner to bid 1♥
1♥	shows 5+ spades	asks partner to bid 1♠
1♠	transfer bid	asks partner to bid 1NT
1NT	8-10 HCP	
2♣	natural 5+ clubs	
2♦	13+ HCP, diamond raise	
2♥/2♠	to Play	
2NT	11-12 HCP	
3♣	10-12 HCP, limit raise in diamonds	

Responses to 2NT* Opening

Responses to 2NT* 5-5 in the minors 5-10 HCP NV and 11-15 HCP Vulnerable

3♣ or 3♦ is to play

3♥* is an asking bid

Opener Rebids

3♠	5-5 minimum (5-10 NV;11-15 VUL)
3NT	maximum
4♣	6-5 (clubs, diamonds), minimum
4♦	6-5 (diamonds, clubs), minimum
4♥	6-5 (clubs, diamonds), maximum
4♠	6-5 (diamonds, clubs), maximum
4NT	6-6 in the minors.

3♠	to play
3NT	to play
4♣/4♦	preemptive bids and to play
4♥/4♠	to play
5♣/5♦	to play

Gambling 3NT* ------ Same as 2/1

Namyats ---------------- Same as 2/1

Shows a hand with 8 - 8 ½ trick in hearts (Open 4♣*), in spades open 4♦*. Refuse transfer by bidding the step in between (4♦ over 4♣ and 4♥ over 4♦), requesting that partner bid an ace if he has one or to sign off in his long suit. 4NT is RKCB.

Responses to 3X Openings

Responses to 3X bids by OPENER (always ensures two of the top three honors Vulnerable) and 5-10 HCP plus distribution. Non-vulnerable at least ONE top Honor.

4♣	Ace asking
4♦	Asks for outside controls first step 0-2 controls (A=2; K=1), second step = 3, etc.
4♥/4♠	to play
4NT	RKCB

SUMMARY- INTERFERENCE BIDS OVER 1♣* OPENING

Direct Seat Interference	
Double – Mathe which shows Majors	
Pass	0-4 HCP
Redouble	5-7 HCP
1♥	8-10 HCP no stopper in hearts
1♠	8-10 HCP no stopper in spades
1NT	8-10 HCP stoppers in the majors
2♣	8-13 HCP and 6+ cards
2♦	8-13 HCP and 6+ diamonds
2♥	11+ spade stopper (no heart stopper)
2♠	11+ heart stopper (no heart stopper)
2NT	11+ both majors stopped

At 1 level – (natural)

Pass	0-4 HCP
Double	5-7 HCP
Suit	8+ HCP, 5+ card suit, Game Force
Jump in suit	10+ HCP, 5/6+ suits, Game Force
1NT	8-13 HCP, with stopper
2NT	10+ HCP, with 1/2 stopper
Cuebid	14+, Game force no stopper

1NT – (natural)

Pass	0-4 HCP
Double	5-7 HCP
Suit	8+ HCP, 5+ card suit

1NT – Mathe which shows Minors

Pass	0-4 HCP
Double	5-7 HCP
2♣	5+ hearts, GF
2♦	5+ spades GF
2♥	5+ HCP, natural and non-forcing
2♠	5+ HCP, natural and non-forcing
3NT	10+ HCP, both minors stopped

At 2 level – (natural)

Pass	0-4 HCP
Double	5-7 HCP
Suit bid	8+ HCP, natural
2NT	10-13 HCP with stopper
3NT	14+ with stoppers

At 3 level – (natural)

Pass	0-4 HCP
Double	5-7 HCP
Suit bid	8+ HCP, and 5+ card suit

At 4 level – (natural)

Pass	0-4 HCP
Double	5-7 HCP, takeout or penalty

Balancing Seat Interference

After 1♣* - (Pass) - 1♦ - (1♥/♠)

Pass	balance minimum no 5-card suit
Double	support for the other 3 suits
Suit Bid	Natural, non-forcing
1NT	shows stopper with (16-21 HCP)
2NT	shows stopper with (22+ HCP)
Cuebid	20 + HCP no stopper

After 1♣* - (Pass) - 1♦ - (1NT for Minors)

Pass	balanced minimum no 5-card suit
Double	support for the both majors
2♣/2♦	unusual extra values shows ♥/♠
2♥/2♠	Natural non-forcing
2NT	shows stopper with (22+ HCP)

After 1♣* - (Pass) - 1♦ - (Double = Majors)

Pass	balanced minimum no 5-card suit
Double	support for the both minors
2♣/2♦	natural 5+ card suit.
2♥/2♠	unusual extra values shows ♣/♦
2NT	shows stopper with (22+ HCP)

INTERFERENCE OVER 1NT by OPPONENTS

Direct Seat = Modified Cappelletti   **Balancing Seat = Modified DONT**
Over strong Club SPAM (1♠ takeout)   **Transfer Lebensohl**

OTHER CONVENTIONAL CALLS

**These are discussed in detail in Timm (2010) "2/1 Game Force a Modern Approach,"
Trafford Press.**

Over a Major Bid Play Leaping Michaels   **Unusual vs. Michaels**
Unusual over Unusual   **Reverse Good-Bad 2NT**
Wolff Sign-Off   **Help Suit Game Try**
4th Suit Forcing to GAME   **Western Cuebid**
Snap Dragon Doubles over a Minor   **Rosencrantz over a Major**
3344 Convention

OVER ANY Other ONE-LEVEL BID BY OPPONENTS

1NT - takeout and shows 8-14 HCP with shortness in bid suit, Double = 15+

LEADS---- 3TH / 5TH vs. suits and 4th Best vs. NOTRUMP

Upside-down COUNT AND ATTITUDE (Suit and Notrump)

Trump Suit Preference